MW01231920

"A Study of Personality Correlates Phobic Reaction among Children's"

ACKNOWLEDGEMENT

It is by the lavish love and blessings of the almighty God, that I have been able o complete my Ph. D thesis successfully hitherto and present this piece of work for which I am eternally indebted.

With sincere regards, I express my heartfelt gratitude to my guide and mentor **Dr.Quadri Syed Javeed, Associate Professor in psychology M.S.S.Arts, Commerce, and Science College, Jalna,** under whose able and scholarly guidance his thesis could not be completed. The guidance and instruction offered by him have accorded me confidence and lent direction to my research work .Working under his guidance has been an enlighting and fulfilling experience for me.

I sincerely thank **Mr.Sontakke Sir (H.O.D. Psychology,Sangmeshor college,Soalapur University) Dr.Ram Sable (S.N.D.T. Women's University, Mumbai)** who allowed me to carry out the present research work and for their constant encouragement during the tenure of my research.

This research would not have been successfully completed without the co-operation and suggestions given by **Dr. Krushna Mastud (MD Psychatry, Barshi Maharashtra)** for his scholarly suggestions who is my inspiration for this research work. I am grateful to **Mr. Hement Sonawane President Niwara Bahuuddeshiy Sansta Barshi, HM Mr. Jadhawar S.L., Niwara Matimand Nivasi Vidyalaya, Barshi Solapur).**

It feels me with inexpressible joy to have got this opportunity express my deep sincere indebtedness gratitude to my father in law Mr. Bhalerao Harishchandra Prabhu parents Shri & Sau. Kaweri Goroba Kamble my borother in law Anand Bhalerao and my brother Rajkumar G. Kamble. My staff member & friends Mr. Jadhav B.A., Mr. Shaikh R.N., Miss. Gaikwad S.S., Mr. Shinde Vitthal, inspiring me o carry out my work with full confidence.

I am also thankful to the faculty member of Psychology Departments & member of Library to their co-operation and timely help to carry out my research work.

I express deep gratitude to my wife Mrs. Vidya Kamble Who supported me in all my academic endeavors. The encouragement and love provided by them have helped me through tough times. Who have taken the brunt of my research always adjusting me to meet deadlines and caring for me.

Last but not the least. I must mention the boom encouragement and seek the forbearance of All through my days accepted the fact that I must complete the task.

Mr. Kamble Dattatraya Goroba

CONTENTS

"A Study of Personality Correlates of Phobic Reactions among Children"

CHAPTER – I

Introduction

Personality psychology

Personality psychology is a branch of psychology that studies personality and individual differences. Its areas of focus include:

- Constructing a coherent picture of a person and his or her major psychological processes
- Investigating individual differences, that is, how people can differ from one another
- Investigating human nature, that is, how all people's behaviour is similar

"Personality" can be defined as a dynamic and organized set of characteristics possessed by a person that uniquely influences his or her cognitions, motivations, and behaviors in various situations. The word "personality" originates from the Latin *persona*, which means mask. Significantly, in the theatre of the ancient Latin-speaking world, the mask was not used as a plot device to *disguise* the identity of a character, but rather was a convention employed to represent or *typify* that character.

The pioneering American psychologist Gordon Allport (1937) described two major ways to study personality: the nomothetic and the idiographic. *Nomothetic psychology* seeks general laws that can be applied to many different people, such as the principle of self-actualization, or the trait of extraversion. *Idiographic psychology* is an attempt to understand the unique aspects of a particular individual.

The study of personality has a broad and varied history in psychology, with an abundance of theoretical traditions. The major theories include dispositional (trait) perspective, psychodynamic, humanistic, biological, behaviorist and social learning perspective. There is no consensus on the definition of "personality" in psychology. Most researchers and psychologists do not explicitly identify themselves with a certain perspective and often take an eclectic approach. Some research is empirically driven such as the "Big 5" personality model whereas other research emphasizes theory development such as psychodynamics. There is also a substantial emphasis on the applied field of personality testing. In psychological education and training, the study of the nature of personality and its psychological development is usually reviewed as a prerequisite to courses in abnormal or clinical psychology.

Philosophical assumptions

Many of the ideas developed by historical and modern personality theorists stem from the basic philosophical assumptions they hold. The study of personality is not a purely empirical discipline, as it brings in elements of art, science, and philosophy to draw general conclusions. The following five categories are some of the most fundamental philosophical assumptions on which theorists disagree:

1. Freedom versus Determinism

This is the debate over whether we have control over our own behavior and understand the motives behind it (Freedom), or if our behavior is causally determined by forces beyond our control (Determinism). Determinism has been considered unconscious, environmental, or biological by various theories.

2. Heredity versus Environment

Personality is thought to be determined largely by genetics and biology, by environment and experiences, or by some combination resulting thereof. There is evidence for all possibilities. Contemporary research suggests that most personality traits are based on the joint influence of genetics and environment. One of the forerunners in this arena is C. Robert Cloninger with the Temperament and Character model.

3. Uniqueness versus Universality

The argument over whether we are all unique individuals (Uniqueness) or if humans are basically similar in their nature (Universality). Gordon Allport, Abraham Maslow, and Carl Rogers were all advocates of the uniqueness of individuals. Behaviorists and cognitive theorists, in contrast, emphasized the importance of universal principles such as reinforcement and self-efficacy.

4. Active versus Reactive

Do we primarily act through our own initiative (Active), or react to outside stimuli (Reactive)? Behavioral theorists typically believe that humans are passively shaped by their environments, whereas humanistic and cognitive theorists believe that humans are more active.

5. Optimistic versus Pessimistic

Personality theories differ on whether people can change their personalities (Optimism), or if they are doomed to remain the same throughout their lives (Pessimism). Theories that place a great deal of emphasis on learning are often, but not always, more optimistic than theories that do not emphasize learning.

Personality theories

Critics of personality theory claim personality is "plastic" across time, places, moods, and situations. Changes in personality may indeed result from diet (or lack thereof), medical effects, significant events, or learning. However, most personality theories emphasize stability over fluctuation. The definition of personality that is most widely supported to date is attributed to the neurologist Paul Roe. He stated personality to be "an individual's predisposition to think certain patterns of thought, and therefore engage in certain patterns of behaviour".

Trait theories

According to the *Diagnostic and Statistical Manual* of the American Psychiatric Association, personality traits are "enduring patterns of perceiving, relating to, and thinking about the environment and oneself that are exhibited in a wide range of social and personal contexts." Theorists generally assume a) traits are relatively stable over time, b) traits differ among individuals (e.g. some people are outgoing while others are reserved), and c) traits influence behavior.

The most common models of traits incorporate three to five broad dimensions or factors. The least controversial dimension, observed as far back as the ancient Greeks, is simply extraversion and introversion (outgoing and physical-stimulation-oriented vs. quiet and physical-stimulation-averse).

- Gordon Allport delineated different kinds of traits, which he also called dispositions. *Central traits* are basic to an individual's personality, while *secondary traits* are more peripheral. *Common traits* are those recognized within a culture and thus may vary from culture to culture. *Cardinal traits* are those by which an individual may be strongly recognized.

- Raymond Cattell's research propagated a two-tiered personality structure with sixteen "primary factors" (16 Personality Factors) and five "secondary factors."

- Hans Eysenck believed just three traits—extraversion, neuroticism and psychoticism—were sufficient to describe human personality. Differences between Cattell and Eysenck emerged due to preferences for different forms of factor analysis, with Cattell using oblique, Eysenck orthogonal rotation to analyse the factors that emerged when personality questionnaires were subjected to statistical analysis. Today, the Big Five factors have the weight of a considerable amount of empirical research behind them, building on the work of Cattell and others.

- Lewis Goldberg proposed a five-dimension personality model, nicknamed the "Big Five":

1. Openness to Experience: the tendency to be imaginative, independent, and interested in variety vs. practical, conforming, and interested in routine.

2. Conscientiousness: the tendency to be organized, careful, and disciplined vs. disorganized, careless, and impulsive.

3. Extraversion: the tendency to be sociable, fun-loving, and affectionate vs. retiring, somber, and reserved.

4. Agreeableness: the tendency to be softhearted, trusting, and helpful vs. ruthless, suspicious, and uncooperative.

5. Neuroticism: the tendency to be calm, secure, and self-satisfied vs. anxious, insecure, and self-pitying

The Big Five contain important dimensions of personality. However, some personality researchers argue that this list of major traits is not exhaustive. Some support has been found for two additional factors: excellent/ordinary and evil/decent. However, no definitive conclusions have been established.

- John L. Holland's *RIASEC* vocational model, commonly referred to as the Holland Codes, stipulates that six personality traits lead people to choose their career paths. In this circumplex model, the six types are represented as a hexagon, with adjacent types more closely related than those more distant. The model is widely used in vocational counseling.

Trait models have been criticized as being purely descriptive and offering little explanation of the underlying causes of personality. Eysenck's theory, however, does propose biological mechanisms as driving traits, and modern behavior genetics researchers have shown a clear genetic substrate to them. Another potential weakness of trait theories is that they may lead some people to accept oversimplified classifications—or worse, offer advice—based on a superficial analysis of personality. Finally, trait models often underestimate the effect of specific situations on people's behavior. It is important to remember that traits are statistical generalizations that do not always correspond to an individual's behavior.

Type theories

Personality type refers to the psychological classification of different types of people. Personality types are distinguished from personality traits, which come in different levels or degrees. For example, according to type theories, there are two types of people, introverts and extraverts. According to trait theories, introversion and extraversion are part of a continuous dimension, with many people in the middle. The idea of psychological types originated in the theoretical work of Carl Jung and William Marston, whose work is reviewed in Dr. Travis Bradberry's *Self-Awareness*. Jung's seminal 1921 book on the subject is available in English as *Psychological Types*.

Building on the writings and observations of Jung, during World War II, Isabel Briggs Myers and her mother, Katharine C. Briggs, delineated personality types by constructing the Myers-Briggs Type Indicator. This model was later used by David Keirsey with a different understanding from Jung, Briggs and Myers. In the former Soviet Union, Lithuanian Aušra Augustinavičiūtė independently derived a model of personality type from Jung's called Socionics.

The model is an older and more theoretical approach to personality, accepting extraversion and introversion as basic psychological orientations in connection with two pairs of psychological functions:

- Perceiving functions: sensing and intuition (trust in concrete, sensory-oriented facts vs. trust in abstract concepts and imagined possibilities)
- Judging functions: thinking and feeling (basing decisions primarily on logic vs. considering the effect on people).

Briggs and Myers also added another personality dimension to their type indicator to measure whether a person prefers to use a judging or perceiving function when interacting with the external world. Therefore they included questions designed to indicate whether someone wishes to come to conclusions (judgment) or to keep options open (perception).[4]

This personality typology has some aspects of a trait theory: it explains people's behaviour in terms of opposite fixed characteristics. In these more traditional models, the sensing/intuition preference is considered the most basic, dividing people into "N" (intuitive) or "S" (sensing) personality types. An "N" is further assumed to be guided either by thinking or feeling, and divided into the "NT" (scientist, engineer) or "NF" (author, humanitarian) temperament. An "S", by contrast, is assumed to be guided more by the judgment/perception axis, and thus divided into the "SJ" (guardian, traditionalist) or "SP" (performer, artisan) temperament. These four are considered basic, with the other two factors in each case (including always extraversion/introversion) less important. Critics of this traditional view have observed that the types can be quite strongly stereotyped by professions (although neither Myers nor Keirsey engaged in such stereotyping in their type descriptions), and thus may arise more from the need to categorize people for purposes of guiding their career choice. This among other objections led to the emergence of the five-factor view, which is less concerned with behavior under work conditions and more concerned with behavior in personal and emotional circumstances. (It should be noted, however, that the MBTI is not designed to measure the "work self", but rather what Myers and McCaulley called the "shoes-off self.") Some critics have argued for more or fewer dimensions while others have proposed entirely different theories (often assuming different definitions of "personality").

Type A and Type B personality theory: During the 1950s, Meyer Friedman and his co-workers defined what they called Type A and Type B behavior patterns. They theorized that intense, hard-driving Type A personalities had a higher risk of coronary disease because they are "stress junkies." Type B people, on the other hand, tended to be relaxed, less competitive, and lower in risk. There was also a Type AB mixed profile. Dr. Redford Williams, cardiologist at Duke University, refuted Friedman's theory that Type A personalities have a higher risk of coronary heart disease; however, current research indicates that only the hostility component of Type A may have health implications. Type A/B theory has been extensively criticized by psychologists because it tends to oversimplify the many dimensions of an individual's personality.

Psychoanalytic theories

Psychoanalytic theories explain human behaviour in terms of the interaction of various components of personality. Sigmund Freud was the founder of this school. Freud drew on the physics of his day (thermodynamics) to coin the term psychodynamics. Based on the idea of converting heat into mechanical energy, he proposed psychic energy could be converted into behavior. Freud's theory places central importance on dynamic, unconscious psychological conflicts.

Freud divides human personality into three significant components: the id, ego, and super-ego. The id acts according to the *pleasure principle*, demanding immediate gratification of its needs regardless of external environment; the ego then must emerge in order to realistically meet the wishes and demands of the id in accordance with the outside world, adhering to the *reality principle*. Finally, the superego(conscience) inculcates moral judgment and societal rules upon the ego, thus forcing the demands of the id to be met not only realistically but morally. The superego is the last function of the personality to develop, and is the embodiment of parental/social ideals established during childhood. According to Freud, personality is based on the dynamic interactions of these three components.

The channeling and release of sexual (libidal) and aggressive energies, which ensues from the "Eros" (sex; instinctual self-preservation) and "Thanatos" (death; instinctual self-annihilation) drives respectively, are major components of his theory. It is important to note that Freud's broad understanding of sexuality included all kinds of pleasurable feelings experienced by the human body.

Freud proposed five psychosexual stages of personality development. He believed adult personality is dependent upon early childhood experiences and largely determined by age five. Fixations that develop during the Infantile stage contribute to adult personality and behavior.

One of Sigmund Freud's earlier associates, Alfred Adler, did agree with Freud early childhood experiences are important to development, and believed birth order may influence personality development. Adler believed the oldest was the one that set high

8

goals to achieve to get the attention they lost back when the younger siblings were born. He believed the middle children were competitive and ambitious possibly so they are able to surpass the first-born's achievements, but were not as much concerned about the glory. He also believed the last born would be more dependent and sociable but be the baby. He also believed that the only child loves being the center of attention and matures quickly, but in the end fails to become independent.

Heinz Kohut thought similarly to Freud's idea of transference. He used narcissism as a model of how we develop our sense of self. Narcissism is the exaggerated sense of one self in which is believed to exist in order to protect one's low self esteem and sense of worthlessness. Kohut had a significant impact on the field by extending Freud's theory of narcissism and introducing what he called the 'self-object transferences' of mirroring and idealization. In other words, children need to idealize and emotionally "sink into" and identify with the idealized competence of admired figures such as parents or older siblings. They also need to have their self-worth mirrored by these people. These experiences allow them to thereby learn the self-soothing and other skills that are necessary for the development of a healthy sense of self.

Another important figure in the world of personality theory was Karen Horney. She is credited with the development of the "real self" and the "ideal self". She believes all people have these two views of their own self. The "real self" is how you really are with regards to personality, values, and morals; but the "ideal self" is a construct you apply to yourself to conform to social and personal norms and goals. Ideal self would be "I can be successful, I am CEO material"; and real self would be "I just work in the mail room, with not much chance of high promotion".

Behaviorist theories

Behaviorists explain personality in terms of the effects external stimuli have on behavior. It was a radical shift away from Freudian philosophy. This school of thought was developed by B. F. Skinner who put forth a model which emphasized the mutual interaction of the person or "the organism" with its environment. Skinner believed children do bad things because the behavior obtains attention that serves as a reinforcer. For example: a child cries because the child's crying in the past has led to attention. These are the *response*, and *consequences*. The response is the child crying, and the attention that child gets is the reinforcing consequence. According to this theory, people's behavior is formed by processes such as operant conditioning. Skinner put forward a "three term contingency model" which helped promote analysis of behavior based on the "Stimulus - Response - Consequence Model" in which the critical question is: "Under which circumstances or antecedent 'stimuli' does the organism engage in a particular behavior or 'response', which in turn produces a particular 'consequence'?"

Richard Herrnstein extended this theory by accounting for attitudes and traits. An attitude develops as the response strength (the tendency to respond) in the presences of a group of stimuli become stable. Rather than describing conditionable traits in non-behavioral language, response strength in a given situation accounts for the environmental portion. Herrstein also saw traits as having a large genetic or biological component as do most modern behaviorists.

Ivan Pavlov is another notable influence. He is well known for his classical conditioning experiments involving dogs. These physiological studies led him to discover the foundation of behaviorism as well as classical conditioning.

Social cognitive theories

In cognitive theory, behavior is explained as guided by cognitions (e.g. expectations) about the world, especially those about other people. Cognitive theories are theories of personality that emphasize cognitive processes such as thinking and judging.

Albert Bandura, a social learning theorist suggested the forces of memory and emotions worked in conjunction with environmental influences. Bandura was known mostly for his "Bobo Doll experiment". During these experiments, Bandura video taped a college student kicking and verbally abusing a bobo doll. He then showed this video to a class of kindergarten children who were getting ready to go out to play. When they entered the play room, they saw bobo dolls, and some hammers. The people observing these children at play saw a group of children beating the doll. He called this study and his findings observational learning, or modeling.

Early examples of approaches to cognitive style are listed by Baron (1982). These include Witkin's (1965) work on field dependency, Gardner's (1953) discovering people had consistent preference for the number of categories they used to categorise heterogeneous objects, and Block and Petersen's (1955) work on confidence in line discrimination judgments. Baron relates early development of cognitive approaches of personality to ego psychology. More central to this field have been:

- Self-efficacy work, dealing with confidence people have in abilities to do tasks;

- Locus of control theory dealing with different beliefs people have about whether their worlds are controlled by themselves or external factors;

- Attributional style theory dealing with different ways in which people explain events in their lives. This approach builds upon locus of control, but extends it by stating we also need to consider whether people attribute to stable causes or variable causes, and to global causes or specific causes.

Various scales have been developed to assess both attributional style and locus of control. Locus of control scales include those used by Rotter and later by Duttweiler, the Nowicki and Strickland (1973) Locus of Control Scale for Children and various locus of control scales specifically in the health domain, most famously that of Kenneth Wallston and his colleagues, The Multidimensional Health Locus of Control Scale. Attributional style has been assessed by the Attributional Style Questionnaire, the Expanded Attributional Style Questionnaire, the Attributions Questionnaire, the Real Events Attributional Style Questionnaire and the Attributional Style Assessment Test.

Walter Mischel (1999) has also defended a cognitive approach to personality. His work refers to "Cognitive Affective Units", and considers factors such as encoding of stimuli, affect, goal-setting, and self-regulatory beliefs. The term "Cognitive Affective Units" shows how his approach considers affect as well as cognition.

11

Personal Construct Psychology (PCP) is a theory of personality developed by the American psychologist George Kelly in the 1950s. From the theory, Kelly derived a psychotherapy approach and also a technique called *The Repertory Grid Interview* that helped his patients to uncover their own "constructs" (defined later) with minimal intervention or interpretation by the therapist. The Repertory Grid was later adapted for various uses within organizations, including decision-making and interpretation of other people's world-views. From his 1963 book, *A Theory of Personality*, pp. 103–104:

- Fundamental Postulate: A person's processes are psychologically channelized by the ways in which the person anticipates events.
- Construction Corollary: A person anticipates events by construing their replications.
- Individuality Corollary: People differ from one another in their construction of events.
- Organization Corollary: Each person characteristically evolves, for convenience in anticipating events, a construction system embracing ordinal relationships between constructs.
- Dichotomy Corollary: A person's construction system is composed of a finite number of dichotomous constructs.
- Choice Corollary: People choose for themselves the particular alternative in a dichotomized construct through which they anticipate the greater possibility for extension and definition of their system.
- Range Corollary: A construct is convenient for the anticipation of a finite range of events only.
- Experience Corollary: A person's construction system varies as the person successively construes the replication of events.
- Modulation Corollary: The variation in a person's construction system is limited by the permeability of the constructs within whose ranges of conveniences the variants lie.
- Fragmentation Corollary: A person may successively employ a variety of construction subsystems which are inferentially incompatible with each other.

- Commonality Corollary: To the extent that one person employs a construction of experience which is similar to that employed by another, the psychological processes of the two individuals are similar to each other.
- Sociality Corollary: To the extent that one person construes another's construction processes, that person may play a role in a social process involving the other person.

Humanistic theories

In humanistic psychology it is emphasized people have free will and they play an active role in determining how they behave. Accordingly, humanistic psychology focuses on subjective experiences of persons as opposed to forced, definitive factors that determine behavior. Abraham Maslow and Carl Rogers were proponents of this view, which is based on the "phenomenal field" theory of Combs and Snygg (1949).

Maslow spent much of his time studying what he called "self-actualizing persons", those who are "fulfilling themselves and doing the best they are capable of doing". Maslow believes all who are interested in growth move towards self-actualizing (growth, happiness, satisfaction) views. Many of these people demonstrate a trend in dimensions of their personalities. Characteristics of self-actualizers according to Maslow include the four key dimensions:

1. Awareness - maintaining constant enjoyment and awe of life. These individuals often experienced a "peak experience". He defined a peak experience as an "intensification of any experience to the degree there is a loss or transcendence of self". A peak experience is one in which an individual perceives an expansion of his or herself, and detects a unity and meaningfulness in life. Intense concentration on an activity one is involved in, such as running a marathon, may invoke a peak experience.
2. Reality and problem centered - they have tendency to be concerned with "problems" in their surroundings.
3. Acceptance/Spontaneity - they accept their surroundings and what cannot be changed.

4. Unhostile sense of humor/democratic - they do not like joking about others, which can be viewed as offensive. They have friends of all backgrounds and religions and hold very close friendships.

Maslow and Rogers emphasized a view of the person as an active, creative, experiencing human being who lives in the present and subjectively responds to current perceptions, relationships, and encounters. They disagree with the dark, pessimistic outlook of those in the Freudian psychoanalysis ranks, but rather view humanistic theories as positive and optimistic proposals which stress the tendency of the human personality toward growth and self-actualization. This progressing self will remain the center of its constantly changing world; a world that will help mold the self but not necessarily confine it. Rather, the self has opportunity for maturation based on its encounters with this world. This understanding attempts to reduce the acceptance of hopeless redundancy. Humanistic therapy typically relies on the client for information of the past and its effect on the present, therefore the client dictates the type of guidance the therapist may initiate. This allows for an individualized approach to therapy. Rogers found patients differ in how they respond to other people. Rogers tried to model a particular approach to therapy- he stressed the reflective or empathetic response. This response type takes the client's viewpoint and reflects back his or her feeling and the context for it. An example of a reflective response would be, "It seems you are feeling anxious about your upcoming marriage". This response type seeks to clarify the therapist's understanding while also encouraging the client to think more deeply and seek to fully understand the feelings they have expressed.

Biopsychological theories

Some of the earliest thinking about possible biological bases of personality grew out of the case of Phineas Gage. In an 1848 accident, a large iron rod was driven through Gage's head, and his personality apparently changed as a result (although descriptionsof these psychological changes are usually exaggerated.

In general, patients with brain damage have been difficult to find and study. In the 1990s, researchers began to use Electroencephalography (EEG), Positron Emission Tomography (PET) and more recently functional Magnetic Resonance Imaging (fMRI), which is now the most widely used imaging technique to help localize personality traits in the brain. One of the founders of this area of brain research is Richard Davidson of the University of Wisconsin–Madison. Davidson's research lab has focused on the role of the prefrontal cortex (PFC) and amygdala in manifesting human personality. In particular, this research has looked at hemispheric asymmetry of activity in these regions. Neuropsychological experiments have suggested that hemispheric asymmetry can affect an individual's personality (particularly in social settings) for individuals with NLD (non-verbal learning disorder), which is marked by the impairment of nonverbal information controlled by the right hemisphere of the brain. Progress will arise in the areas of gross motor skills, inability to organize visual-spatial relations, or adapt to novel social situations. Frequently, a person with NLD is unable to interpret non-verbal cues, and therefore experiences difficulty interacting with peers in socially normative ways.

One integrative, biopsychosocial approach to personality and psychopathology, linking brain and environmental factors to specific types of activity, is the hypostatic model of personality, created by Codrin Stefan Tapu.

Personality tests

There are two major types of personality tests. Projective tests assume personality is primarily unconscious and assess an individual by how he or she responds to an ambiguous stimulus, like an ink blot. The idea is unconscious needs will come out in the person's response, e.g. an aggressive person may see images of destruction. Objective tests assume personality is consciously accessible and measure it by self-report questionnaires. Research on psychological assessment has generally found objective tests are more valid and reliable than projective tests.

- Forte Communication Style Profile
- Holland Codes
- Keirsey Temperament Sorter
- Kelly's Repertory Grid
- Minnesota Multiphasic Personality Inventory
- Morrisby Profile

- Myers-Briggs Type Indicator
- NEO PI-R
- Personality Assessment Inventory
- ProScan Survey by PDP
- Rorschach test
- Thematic Apperception Test

Personality and inner experience

Psychology has traditionally defined personality through behavioral patterns, and more recently with neuroscientific study of the brain. In recent years, some psychologists have turned to the study of inner experiences for insight into personality and individuality. Russel Hurlburt, a psychologist at the University of Nevada, Las Vegas has studied personality by having individuals record their individual experiences at random times throughout the day. In analyzing the mental freeze-frames that his subjects report, he has found significant variation in inner mental life, and several correlations with behavioral patterns.

Psychosexual development

In Freudian psychology, psychosexual development is a central element of the psychoanalytic sexual drive theory, that human beings, from birth, possess an instinctual libido (sexual appetite) that develops in five stages. Each stage — the oral, the anal, the phallic, the latent, and the genital — is characterized by the erogenous zone that is the source of the libidinal drive. Sigmund Freud proposed that if the child experienced anxiety, thwarting his or her sexual appetite during any libidinal (psychosexual) development stage, said anxiety would persist into adulthood as a neurosis, a functional mental disorder.

Freudian psychosexual development

Sexual infantilism — In pursuing and satisfying his or her libido (sexual drive), the child might experience failure (parental and societal disapproval) and thus might associate anxiety with the given erogenous zone. To avoid anxiety, the child becomes fixated, preoccupied with the psychologic themes related to the erogenous zone in question, which persist into adulthood, and underlie the personality and psychopathology of the man or woman, as neurosis, hysteria, personality disorders, et cetera.

Stage	Age Range	Erogenous zone	Consequences of psychologic fixation
Oral	Birth–1 year	Mouth	Orally aggressive: chewing gum and the ends of pencils, etc. Orally Passive: smoking, eating, kissing, oral sexual practices Oral stage fixation might result in a passive, gullible, immature, manipulative personality.
Anal	1–3 years	Bowel and bladder elimination	Anal retentive: Obsessively organized, or excessively neat Anal expulsive: reckless, careless, defiant, disorganized, coprophiliac
Phallic	3–6 years	Genitalia	Oedipus complex (in boys) Electra complex (in girls)
Latency	6–puberty	Dormant sexual feelings	Sexual unfulfillment if fixation occurs in this stage.
Genital	Puberty–death	Sexual interests mature	Frigidity, impotence, unsatisfactory relationships

Oral stage

The first stage of psychosexual development is the oral stage, spanning from birth until the age of two years, wherein the infant's mouth is the focus of libidinal gratification derived from the pleasure of feeding at the mother's breast, and from the oral exploration of his or her environment, i.e. the tendency to place objects in the mouth. The id dominates, because neither the ego nor the super ego is yet fully developed, and, since the infant has no personality (identity), every action is based upon the pleasure principle. Nonetheless, the infantile ego is forming during the oral stage; two factors contribute to its formation: (i) in developing a body image, he or she is discrete from the external world, e.g. the child understands pain when it is applied to his or her body, thus identifying the physical boundaries between body and environment; (ii) experiencing delayed gratification leads to understanding that specific behaviors satisfy some needs, e.g. crying gratifies certain needs.

Weaning is the key experience in the infant's oral stage of psychosexual development, his or her first feeling of loss consequent to losing the physical intimacy of feeding at mother's breast. Yet, weaning increases the infant's self-awareness that he or she does not control the environment, and thus learns of delayed gratification, which leads to the formation of the capacities for independence (awareness of the limits of the self) and trust (behaviors leading to gratification). Yet, thwarting of the oral-stage — too much or too little gratification of desire — might lead to an oral-stage fixation, characterised by passivity, gullibility, immaturity, unrealistic optimism, which is manifested in a manipulative personality consequent to ego malformation. In the case of too much gratification, the child does not learn that he or she does not control the environment, and that gratification is not always immediate, thereby forming an immature personality. In the case of too little gratification, the infant might become passive upon learning that gratification is not forthcoming, despite having produced the gratifying behavior.

Anal stage

The second stage of psychosexual development is the anal stage, spanning from the age of fifteen months to three years, wherein the infant's erogenous zone changes from the mouth (the upper digestive tract) to the anus (the lower digestive tract), while the ego formation continues. Toilet training is the child's key anal-stage experience, occurring at about the age of two years, and results in conflict between the Id (demanding immediate gratification) and the Ego (demanding delayed gratification) in eliminating bodily wastes, and handling related activities (e.g. manipulating feces, coping with parental demands). The style of parenting influences the resolution of the Id–Ego conflict, which can be either gradual and psychologically uneventful, or which can be sudden and psychologically traumatic. The ideal resolution of the Id–Ego conflict is in the child's adjusting to moderate parental demands that teach the value and importance of physical cleanliness and environmental order, thus producing a self-controlled adult. Yet, if the parents make immoderate demands of the child, by over-emphasizing toilet training, it might lead to the development of a compulsive personality, a person too concerned with neatness and order. If the child obeys the Id, and the parents yield, he or she might develop a self-indulgent personality characterized by personal slovenliness and environmental disorder. If the parents respond to that, the child must comply, but might develop a weak sense of Self, because it was the parents' will, and not the child's ego, who controlled the toilet training.

Phallic stage

The third stage of psychosexual development is the phallic stage, spanning the ages of three to six years, wherein the child's genitalia are his or her primary erogenous zone. It is in this third infantile development stage that children become aware of their bodies, the bodies of other children, and the bodies of their parents; they gratify physical curiosity by undressing and exploring each other and their genitals, and so learn the physical (sexual) differences between "male" and "female" and the gender differences between "boy" and "girl". In the phallic stage, a boy's decisive psychosexual experience is the Oedipus complex, his son–father competition for possession of mother. This psychological complex derives from the 5th-century BC Greek mythologic character Oedipus, who unwittingly killed his father, Laius, and sexually possessed his mother, Jocasta. Analogously, in the phallic stage, a girl's decisive psychosexual experience is the Electra complex, her daughter–mother competition for psychosexual possession of father. This psychological complex derives from the 5th-century BC Greek mythologic Electra, who plotted matricidal revenge with Orestes, her brother, against Clytemnestra, their mother, and Aegisthus, their stepfather, for their murder of Agamemnon, their father, (cf. *Electra*, by Sophocles).

Initially, Freud equally applied the Oedipus complex to the psychosexual development of boys and girls, but later developed the female aspects of the theory as the feminine Oedipus attitude and the negative Oedipus complex; yet, it was his student–collaborator, Carl Jung, who coined the term Electra complex in 1913. Nonetheless, Freud rejected Jung's term as psychoanalytically inaccurate: "that what we have said about the Oedipus complex applies with complete strictness to the male child only, and that we are right in rejecting the term 'Electra complex', which seeks to emphasize the analogy between the attitude of the two sexes".

Oedipus — Despite mother being the parent who primarily gratifies the child's desires, the child begins forming a discrete sexual identity — "boy", "girl" — that alters the dynamics of the parent and child relationship; the parents become the focus of infantile libidinal energy. The boy focuses his libido (sexual desire) upon his mother, and focuses jealousy and emotional rivalry against his father — because it is he who sleeps with mother. To facilitate uniting him with his mother, the boy's id wants to kill father (as did Oedipus), but the ego, pragmatically based upon the reality principle, knows that the father is the stronger of the two males competing to possess the one female. Nevertheless, the boy remains ambivalent about his father's place in the family, which is manifested as fear of castration by the physically greater father; the fear is an irrational, subconscious manifestation of the infantile Id.

Electra — Whereas boys develop castration anxiety, girls develop penis envy that is rooted in anatomic fact: without a penis, she cannot sexually possess mother, as the infantile id demands. Resultantly, the girl redirects her desire for sexual union upon father; thus, she progresses towards heterosexual femininity that culminates in bearing a child who replaces the absent penis. Moreover, after the phallic stage, the girl's psychosexual development includes transferring her primary erogenous zone from the infantile clitoris to the adult vagina. Freud thus considered a girl's Oedipal conflict to be more emotionally intense than that of a boy, resulting, potentially, in a submissive woman of insecure personality.

Psychologic defense — In both sexes, defense mechanisms provide transitory resolutions of the conflict between the drives of the Id and the drives of the Ego. The first defense mechanism is repression, the blocking of memories, emotional impulses, and ideas from the conscious mind; yet it does not resolve the Id–Ego conflict. The second defense mechanism is identification, by which the child incorporates, to his or her ego, the personality characteristics of the same-sex parent; in so adapting, the boy diminishes his castration anxiety, because his likeness to father protects him from father's wrath as a rival for mother; by so adapting, the girl facilitates identifying with mother, who understands that, in being females, neither of them possesses a penis, and thus they are not antagonists.

Dénouement — Unresolved psychosexual competition for the opposite-sex parent might produce a phallic-stage fixation leading a girl to become a woman who continually strives to dominate men (viz. penis envy), either as an unusually seductive woman (high self-esteem) or as an unusually submissive woman (low self-esteem). In a boy, a phallic-stage fixation might lead him to become an aggressive, over-ambitious, vain man. Therefore, the satisfactory parental handling and resolution of the Oedipus complex and of the Electra complex are most important in developing the infantile super-ego, because, by identifying with a parent, the child internalizes morality, thereby, choosing to comply with societal rules, rather than having to reflexively comply in fear of punishment.

Latency stage

The fourth stage of psychosexual development is the latency stage that spans from the age of six years until puberty, wherein the child consolidates the character habits he or she developed in the three, earlier stages of psychologic and sexual development. Whether or not the child has successfully resolved the Oedipal conflict, the instinctual drives of the id are inaccessible to the Ego, because his or her defense mechanisms repressed them during the phallic stage. Hence, because said drives are latent (hidden) and gratification is delayed — unlike during the preceding oral, anal, and phallic stages — the child must derive the pleasure of gratification from secondary process-thinking that directs the libidinal drives towards external activities, such as schooling, friendships, hobbies, et cetera. Any neuroses established during the fourth, latent stage, of psychosexual development might derive from the inadequate resolution either of the Oedipus conflict or of the Ego's failure to direct his or her energies towards socially acceptable activities.

Genital stage

The fifth stage of psychosexual development is the genital stage that spans puberty and adult life, and thus occupies most of the life of a man and of a woman; its purpose is the psychologic detachment and independence from the parents. The genital stage affords the person the ability to confront and resolve his or her remaining psychosexual childhood conflicts. As in the phallic stage, the genital stage is centered upon the genitalia, but the sexuality is consensual and adult, rather than solitary and infantile. The psychological difference between the phallic and genital stages is that the ego is established in the latter; the person's concern shifts from primary-drive gratification (instinct) to applying secondary process-thinking to gratify desire symbolically and intellectually by means of friendships, a love relationship, family and adult responsibilities.

Criticism

Feminist

Contemporaneously, Sigmund Freud's psychosexual development theory is criticized as sexist, because it was informed with his introspection (self-analysis). To integrate the female libido (sexual desire) to psychosexual development, he proposed that girls develop "penis envy". In response, the German Neo-Freudian psychoanalyst Karen Horney, counter-proposed that girls instead develop "Power envy", rather than penis envy. She further proposed the concept of "womb and vagina envy", the male's envy of the female ability to bear children; yet, contemporary formulations further develop said envy from the biologic (child-bearing) to the psychologic (nurturance), envy of women's perceived right to be the kind parent.

Scientific

A usual criticism of the scientific (experimental) validity of the Freudian psychology theory of human psychosexual development is that Sigmund Freud (1856–1939) was personally fixated upon human sexuality, therefore, he favored defining human development with a normative theory of psychologic and sexual development. Hence, the phallic stage proved controversial, for being based upon clinical observations of the Oedipus complex.

In *Analysis of a Phobia in a Five-year-old Boy* (1909), the case study of the boy "Little Hans" (Herbert Graf, 1903–73) who was afflicted with equinophobia. The relation between Hans's fears — of horses and of father — derived from external factors, the birth of a sister, and internal factors, the desire of the infantile id to replace father as companion to mother, and guilt for enjoying the masturbation normal to a boy of his age. Moreover, his admitting to wanting to procreate with mother was considered proof of the boy's sexual attraction to the opposite-sex parent; he was a heterosexual male. Yet, the boy Hans was unable to relate fearing horses to fearing his father. The psychoanalyst Freud noted that "Hans had to be told many things that he could not say himself" and that "he had to be presented with thoughts, which he had, so far, shown no signs of possessing".

Anthropologic

Contemporary criticism also questions the universality of the Freudian theory of personality (Id, Ego, Super-ego) discussed in the essay *On Narcissism* (1917), wherein he said that "it is impossible to suppose that a unity, comparable to the ego can exist in the individual from the very start". Contemporary cultural considerations have questioned the normative presumptions of the Freudian psychodynamic perspective that posits the son–father conflict of the Oedipal complex as universal and essential to human psychologic development.

The anthropologist Bronisław Malinowski's studies of the Trobriand islanders challenged the Freudian proposal that psychosexual development (e.g. the Oedipus complex) was universal. He reported that in the insular matriarchal society of the

23

Trobriand, boys are disciplined by their maternal uncles, not their fathers; impartial, avuncular discipline. In *Sex and Repression in Savage Society* (1927), Malinowski reported that boys dreamed of feared uncles, not of beloved fathers, thus, Power — not sexual jealousy — is the source of Oedipal conflict in such non–Western societies. In *Human Behavior in Global Perspective: an Introduction to Cross-Cultural Psychology* (1999), Marshall H. Segall et al. propose that Freud based the theory of psychosexual development upon a misinterpretation. Furthermore, contemporary research confirms that although personality traits corresponding to the oral stage, the anal stage, the phallic stage, the latent stage, and the genital stage are observable, they remain undetermined as fixed stages of childhood, and as adult personality traits derived from childhood.

KAREN HORNEY (1885 - 1952)

Horney's theory is perhaps the best theory of neurosis we have. First, she offered a different way of viewing neurosis. She saw it as much more continuous with normal life than previous theorists. Specifically, she saw neurosis as an attempt to make life bearable, as a way of "interpersonal control and coping." This is, of course, what we all strive to do on a day-to-day basis, only most of us seem to be doing alright, while the neurotic seems to be sinking fast.

In her clinical experience, she discerned ten particular patterns of neurotic needs. They are based on things that we all need, but they have become distorted in several ways by the difficulties of some people's lives:

Let's take the first need, for affection and approval, as an example. We all need affection, so what makes such a need neurotic? First, the need is unrealistic, unreasonable, indiscriminate. For example, we all need affection, but we don't expect it from everyone we meet. We don't expect great outpourings of affection from even our close friends and relations. We don't expect our loved ones to show affection at all times, in all circumstances. We don't expect great shows of love while our partners are filing out tax forms, for example. And, we realize that there may be times in our lives where we have to be self-sufficient.

24

Second, the neurotic's need is much more intense, and he or she will experience great anxiety if the need is not met, or if it even appears that it may not be met in the future. It is this, of course, that leads to the unrealistic nature of the need. Affection, to continue the example, has to be shown clearly at all times, in all circumstances, by all people, or the panic sets in. The neurotic has made the need too central to their existence.

The neurotic needs are as follows:

1. The neurotic need for affection and approval, the indiscriminate need to please others and be liked by them.

2. The neurotic need for a partner, for someone who will take over one's life. This includes the idea that love will solve all of one's problems. Again, we all would like a partner to share life with, but the neurotic goes a step or two too far.

3. The neurotic need to restrict one's life to narrow borders, to be undemanding, satisfied with little, to be inconspicuous. Even this has its normal counterpart. Who hasn't felt the need to simplify life when it gets too stressful, to join a monastic order, disappear into routine, or to return to the womb?

4. The neurotic need for power, for control over others, for a facade of omnipotence. We all seek strength, but the neurotic may be desperate for it. This is dominance for its own sake, often accompanied by a contempt for the weak and a strong belief in one's own rational powers.

5. The neurotic need to exploit others and get the better of them. In the ordinary person, this might be the need to have an effect, to have impact, to be heard. In the neurotic, it can become manipulation and the belief that people are there to be used. It may also involve a fear of being used, of looking stupid. You may have noticed that the people who love practical jokes more often than not cannot take being the butt of such a joke themselves!

6. The neurotic need for social recognition or prestige. We are social creatures, and sexual ones, and like to be appreciated. But these people are overwhelmingly

concerned with appearances and popularity. They fear being ignored, be thought plain, "uncool," or "out of it."

7. The neurotic need for personal admiration. We need to be admired for inner qualities as well as outer ones. We need to feel important and valued. But some people are more desperate, and need to remind everyone of their importance -- "Nobody recognizes genius," "I'm the real power behind the scenes, you know," and so on. Their fear is of being thought nobodies, unimportant and meaningless.

8. The neurotic need for personal achievement. Again, there is nothing intrinsically wrong with achievement -- far from it! But some people are obsessed with it. They have to be number one at everything they do. Since this is, of course, quite a difficult task, you will find these people devaluing anything they cannot be number one in! If they are good runners, then the discus and the hammer are "side shows." If academic abilities are their strength, physical abilities are of no importance, and so on.

9. The neurotic need for self-sufficiency and independence. We should all cultivate some autonomy, but some people feel that they shouldn't ever need anybody. They tend to refuse help and are often reluctant to commit to a relationship.

10. The neurotic need for perfection and unassailability. To become better and better at life and our special interests is hardly neurotic, but some people are driven to be perfect and scared of being flawed. They can't be caught making a mistake and need to be in control at all times.

As Horney investigated these neurotic needs, she began to recognize that they can be clustered into three broad coping strategies:

I. Compliance, which includes needs one, two, and three.

II. Aggression, including needs four through eight.

III. Withdrawal, including needs nine, ten, and three. She added three here because it is crucial to the illusion of total independence and perfection that you limit the breadth of your life!

In her writings, she used a number of other phrases to refer to these three strategies. Besides compliance, she referred to the first as the moving-toward strategy and the self-effacing solution. One should also note that it is the same as Adler's getting or leaning approach, or the phlegmatic personality.

Besides aggression, the second was referred to as moving-against and the expansive solution. It is the same as Alder's ruling or dominant type, or the choleric personality.

And, besides withdrawal, she called the third moving-away-from and the resigning solution. It is somewhat like Adler's avoiding type, the melancholy personality.

Development

It is true that some people who are abused or neglected as children suffer from neuroses as adults. What we often forget is that most do not. If you have a violent father, or a schizophrenic mother, or are sexually molested by a strange uncle, you may nevertheless have other family members that love you, take care of you, and work to protect you from further injury, and you will grow up to be a healthy, happy adult. It is even more true that the great majority of adult neurotics did not in fact suffer from childhood neglect or abuse! So the question becomes, if it is not neglect or abuse that causes neurosis, what does?

Horney's answer, which she called the "basic evil," is parental indifference, a lack of warmth and affection in childhood. Even occasional beatings or an early sexual experience can be overcome, if the child feels wanted and loved.

The key to understanding parental indifference is that it is a matter of the child's perception, and not the parents' intentions. "The road to hell," it might pay to remember, "is paved with good intentions." A well-intentioned parent may easily communicate indifference to children with such things as showing a preference for one child over another, blaming a child for what they may not have done, overindulging one moment and rejecting another, neglecting to fulfill promises, disturbing a child's friendships, making fun of a child's thinking, and so on. Please notice that many parents -- even good ones -- find themselves doing these things because of the many pressures they may be under. Other parents do these things because they themselves are neurotic, and place their own needs ahead of their children's

Horney noticed that, in contrast to our stereotypes of children as weak and passive, their first reaction to parental indifference is anger, a response she calls basic hostility. To be frustrated first leads to an effort at protesting the injustice!

Some children find this hostility effective, and over time it becomes a habitual response to life's difficulties. In other words, they develop an aggressive coping strategy. They say to themselves, "If I have power, no one can hurt me."

Most children, however, find themselves overwhelmed by basic anxiety, which in children is mostly a matter of fear of helplessness and abandonment. For survival's sake, basic hostility must be suppressed and the parents won over. If this seems to work better for the child, it may become the preferred coping strategy -- compliance. They say to themselves, "If I can make you love me, you will not hurt me."

Some children find that neither aggression nor compliance eliminate the perceived parental indifference. They "solve" the problem by withdrawing from family involvement into themselves, eventually becoming sufficient unto themselves -- the third coping strategy. They say, "If I withdraw, nothing can hurt me."

Self theory

Horney had one more way of looking at neurosis -- in terms of self images. For Horney, the self is the core of your being, your potential. If you were healthy, you would have an accurate conception of who you are, and you would then be free to realize that potential (self-realization).

The neurotic has a different view of things. The neurotics self is "split" into a despised self and an ideal self. Other theorists postulate a "looking-glass" self, the you you think others see. If you look around and see (accurately or not) others despising you, then you take that inside you as what you assume is the real you. On the other hand, if you are lacking in some way, that implies there are certain ideals you should be living up to. You create an ideal self out of these "shoulds." Understand that the ideal self is not a positive goal; it is unrealistic and ultimately impossible. So the neurotic swings back and forth between hating themselves and pretending to be perfect.

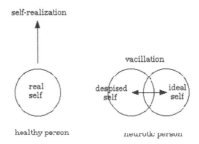

Horney described this stretching between the despised and ideal selves as "the tyranny of the shoulds" and neurotic "striving for glory:"

The compliant person believes "I should be sweet, self-sacrificing, saintly." The aggressive person says "I should be powerful, recognized, a winner." The withdrawing person believes "I should be independent, aloof, perfect."

And while vacillating between these two impossible selves, the neurotic is alienated from their true core and prevented from actualizing their potentials.

JEAN PIAGET (1896 – 1980)

Jean Piaget began his career as a biologist -- specifically, a malacologist! But his interest in science and the history of science soon overtook his interest in snails and clams. As he delved deeper into the thought-processes of doing science, he became interested in the nature of thought itself, especially in the development of thinking. Finding relatively little work done in the area, he had the opportunity to give it a label. He called it genetic epistemology, meaning the study of the development of knowledge.

He noticed, for example, that even infants have certain skills in regard to objects in their environment. These skills were certainly simple ones, sensori-motor skills, but they directed the way in which the infant explored his or her environment and so how they gained more knowledge of the world and more sophisticated exploratory skills. These skills he called schemas.

For example, an infant knows how to grab his favorite rattle and thrust it into his mouth. He's got that schema down pat. When he comes across some other object -- say daddy's expensive watch, he easily learns to transfer his "grab and thrust" schema to the new object. This Piaget called assimilation, specifically assimilating a new object into an old schema.

When our infant comes across another object again -- say a beach ball -- he will try his old schema of grab and thrust. This of course works poorly with the new object. So the schema will adapt to the new object: Perhaps, in this example, "squeeze and drool" would be an appropriate title for the new schema. This is called accommodation, specifically accomodating an old schema to a new object.

Assimilation and accommodation are the two sides of adaptation, Piaget's term for what most of us would call learning. Piaget saw adaptation, however, as a good deal broader than the kind of learning that Behaviorists in the US were talking about. He saw it as a fundamentally biological process. Even one's grip has to accommodate to a stone, while clay is assimilated into our grip. All living things adapt, even without a nervous system or brain.

Assimilation and accommodation work like pendulum swings at advancing our understanding of the world and our competency in it. According to Piaget, they are directed at a balance between the structure of the mind and the environment, at a certain congruency between the two, that would indicate that you have a good (or at least good-enough) model of the universe. This ideal state he calls equilibrium.

As he continued his investigation of children, he noted that there were periods where assimilation dominated, periods where accommodation dominated, and periods of relative equilibrium, and that these periods were similar among all the children he looked at in their nature and their timing. And so he developed the idea of stages of cognitive development. These constitute a lasting contribution to psychology.

The sensor motor stage

The first stage, to which we have already referred, is the sensorimotor stage. It lasts from birth to about two years old. As the name implies, the infant uses senses and motor abilities to understand the world, beginning with reflexes and ending with complex combinations of sensorimotor skills.

Between one and four months, the child works on primary circular reactions -- just an action of his own which serves as a stimulus to which it responds with the same action, and around and around we go. For example, the baby may suck her thumb. That feels good, so she sucks some more... Or she may blow a bubble. That's interesting so I'll do it again....

Between four and 12 months, the infant turns to secondary circular reactions, which involve an act that extends out to the environment: She may squeeze a rubber duckie. It goes "quack." That's great, so do it again, and again, and again. She is learning "procedures that make interesting things last."

At this point, other things begin to show up as well. For example, babies become ticklish, although they must be aware that someone else is tickling them or it won't work. And they begin to develop object permanence. This is the ability to recognize that, just because you can't see something doesn't mean it's gone! Younger infants seem to function by an "out of sight, out of mind" schema. Older infants remember, and may even try to find things they can no longer see.

Between 12 months and 24 months, the child works on tertiary circular reactions. They consist of the same "making interesting things last" cycle, except with constant variation. I hit the drum with the stick -- rat-tat-tat-tat. I hit the block with the stick -- thump-thump. I hit the table with the stick -- clunk-clunk. I hit daddy with the stick -- ouch-ouch. This kind of active experimentation is best seen during feeding time, when discovering new and interesting ways of throwing your spoon, dish, and food.

Around one and a half, the child is clearly developing mental representation, that is, the ability to hold an image in their mind for a period beyond the immediate experience. For example, they can engage in deferred imitation, such as throwing a tantrum after seeing one an hour ago. They can use mental combinations to solve simple problems, such as putting down a toy in order to open a door. And they get good at pretending. Instead of using dollies essentially as something to sit at, suck on, or throw, now the child will sing to it, tuck it into bed, and so on.

Preoperational stage

The preoperational stage lasts from about two to about seven years old. Now that the child has mental representations and is able to pretend, it is a short step to the use of symbols.

A symbol is a thing that represents something else. A drawing, a written word, or a spoken word comes to be understood as representing a real dog. The use of language is, of course, the prime example, but another good example of symbol use is creative play, wherein checkers are cookies, papers are dishes, a box is the table, and so on. By manipulating symbols, we are essentially thinking, in a way the infant could not: in the absence of the actual objects involved!

Along with symbolization, there is a clear understanding of past and future. for example, if a child is crying for its mother, and you say "Mommy will be home soon," it will now tend to stop crying. Or if you ask him, "Remember when you fell down?" he will respond by making a sad face.

On the other hand, the child is quite egocentric during this stage, that is, he sees things pretty much from one point of view: his own! She may hold up a picture so only she can see it and expect you to see it too. Or she may explain that grass grows so she won't get hurt when she falls.

Piaget did a study to investigate this phenomenon called the mountains study. He would put children in front of a simple plaster mountain range and seat himself to the side, then ask them to pick from four pictures the view that he, Piaget, would see. Younger children would pick the picture of the view they themselves saw; older kids picked correctly.

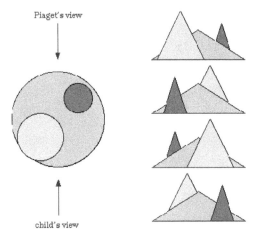

Piaget's view

child's view

Similarly, younger children center on one aspect of any problem or communication at a time. for example, they may not understand you when you tell them "Your father is my husband." Or they may say things like "I don't live in the USA; I live in Pennsylvania!" Or, if you show them five black and three white marbles and ask them "Are there more marbles or more black marbles?" they will respond "More black ones!"

Perhaps the most famous example of the preoperational child's centrism is what Piaget refers to as their inability to conserve liquid volume. If I give a three year old some chocolate milk in a tall skinny glass, and I give myself a whole lot more in a short fat glass, she will tend to focus on only one of the dimensions of the glass. Since the milk in the tall skinny glass goes up much higher, she is likely to assume that there is more milk in that one than in the short fat glass, even though there is far more in the latter. It is the development of the child's ability to decenter that marks him as havingmoved to the next stage.

Concrete operations stage

The concrete operations stage lasts from about seven to about 11. The word operations refers to logical operations or principles we use when solving problems. In this stage, the child not only uses symbols representationally, but can manipulate those symbols logically. Quite an accomplishment! But, at this point, they must still perform these operations within the context of concrete situations.

The stage begins with progressive decentering. By six or seven, most children develop the ability to conserve number, length, and liquid volume. Conservation refers to the idea that a quantity remains the same despite changes in appearance. If you show a child four marbles in a row, then spread them out, the preoperational child will focus on the spread, and tend to believe that there are now more marbles than before.

Or if you have two five inch sticks laid parallel to each other, then move one of them a little, she may believe that the moved stick is now longer than the other.

The concrete operations child, on the other hand, will know that there are still four marbles, and that the stick doesn't change length even though it now extends beyond the other. And he will know that you have to look at more than just the height of the milk in the glass: If you pour the mild from the short, fat glass into the tall, skinny glass, he will tell you that there is the same amount of milk as before, despite the dramatic increase in mild-level!

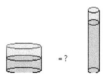

By seven or eight years old, children develop conservation of substance: If I take a ball of clay and roll it into a long thin rod, or even split it into ten little pieces, the child knows that there is still the same amount of clay. And he will know that, if you rolled it all back into a single ball, it would look quite the same as it did -- a feature known as reversibility.

By nine or ten, the last of the conservation tests is mastered: conservation of area. If you take four one-inch square pieces of felt, and lay them on a six-by-six cloth together in the center, the child who conserves will know that they take up just as much room as the same squares spread out in the corners, or, for that matter, anywhere at all.

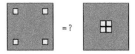

If all this sounds too easy to be such a big deal, test your friends on conservation of mass: Which is heavier: a million tons of lead, or a million tons of feathers?

In addition, a child learns classification and seriation during this stage. Classification refers back to the question of whether there are more marbles or more black marbles? Now the child begins to get the idea that one set can include another. Seriation is putting things in order. The younger child may start putting things in order by, say, size, but will quickly lose track. Now the child has no problem with such a task. Since arithmetic is essentially nothing more than classification and seriation, the child is now ready for some formal education!

Formal operations stage

But the concrete operations child has a hard time applying his new-found logical abilities to non-concrete -- i.e. abstract -- events. If mom says to junior "You shouldn't make fun of that boy's nose. How would you feel if someone did that to you?" he is likely to respond "I don't have a big nose!" Even this simple lesson may well be too abstract, too hypothetical, for his kind of thinking.

Don't judge the concrete operations child too harshly, though. Even adults are often taken-aback when we present them with something hypothetical: "If Edith has a lighter complexion than Susan, and Edith is darker than Lily, who is the darkest?" Most people need a moment or two.

From around 12 on, we enter the formal operations stage. Here we become increasingly competent at adult-style thinking. This involves using logical operations, and using them in the abstract, rather than the concrete. We often call this hypothetical thinking.

Here's a simple example of a task that a concrete operations child couldn't do, but which a formal operations teenager or adult could -- with a little time and effort. Consider this rule about a set of cards that have letters on one side and numbers on the other: "If a card has a vowel on one side, then it has an even number on the other side." Take a look at the cards below and tell me, which cards do I need to turn over to tell if this rule is actually true? You'll find the answer at the end of this chapter.

It is the formal operations stage that allows one to investigate a problem in a careful and systematic fashion. Ask a 16 year old to tell you the rules for making pendulums swing quickly or slowly, and he may proceed like this:

His experiment -- and it is an experiment -- would tell him that a short string leads to a fast swing, and a long string to a slow swing, and that the weight of the pendulum means nothing at all!

The teenager has learned to group possibilities in four different ways:

By conjunction: "Both A and B make a difference" (e.g. both the string's length and the pendulum's weight).

By disjunction: "It's either this or that" (e.g. it's either the length or the weight).

By implication: "If it's this, then that will happen" (the formation of a hypothesis).

By incompatibility: "When this happens, that doesn't" (the elimination of a hypothesis).

On top of that, he can operate on the operations -- a higher level of grouping. If you have a proposition, such as "it could be the string or the weight," you can do four things with it:

Identity: Leave it alone. "It could be the string or the weight."

Negation: Negate the components and replace or's with and's (and vice versa). "It might not be the string and not the weight, either."

Reciprocity: Negate the components but keep the and's and or's as they are. "Either it is not the weight or it is not the string."

Correlativity: Keep the components as they are, but replace or's with and's, etc. "It's the weight and the string."

Erikson

Erikson is a Freudian ego-psychologist. This means that he accepts Freud's ideas as basically correct, including the more debatable ideas such as the Oedipal complex, and accepts as well the ideas about the ego that were added by other Freudian loyalists such as Heinz Hartmann and, of, course, Anna Freud. However, Erikson is much more society and culture-oriented than most Freudians, as you might expect from someone with his anthropological interests, and he often pushes the instincts and the unconscious practically out of the picture. Perhaps because of this, Erikson is popular among Freudians and non-Freudians alike!

The epigenetic principle

He is most famous for his work in refining and expanding Freud's theory of stages. Development, he says, functions by the epigenetic principle. This principle says that we develop through a predetermined unfolding of our personalities in eight stages. Our progress through each stage is in part determined by our success, or lack of success, in all the previous stages. A little like the unfolding of a rose bud, each petal opens up at a certain time, in a certain order, which nature, through its genetics, has determined. If we interfere in the natural order of development by pulling a petal forward prematurely or out of order, we ruin the development of the entire flower.

Each stage involves certain developmental tasks that are psychosocial in nature. Although he follows Freudian tradition by calling them crises, they are more drawn out and less specific than that term implies. The child in grammar school, for example, has to learn to be industrious during that period of his or her life, and that industriousness is learned through the complex social interactions of school and family.

The various tasks are referred to by two terms. The infant's task, for example, is called "trust-mistrust." At first, it might seem obvious that the infant must learn trust and not mistrust. But Erikson made it clear that there it is a balance we must learn: Certainly, we need to learn mostly trust; but we also need to learn a little mistrust, so as not to grow up to become gullible fools!

Each stage has a certain optimal time as well. It is no use trying to rush children into adulthood, as is so common among people who are obsessed with success. Neither is it possible to slow the pace or to try to protect our children from the demands of life. There is a time for each task.

If a stage is managed well, we carry away a certain virtue or psychosocial strength which will help us through the rest of the stages of our lives. On the other hand, if we don't do so well, we may develop maladaptations and malignancies, as well as endanger all our future development. A malignancy is the worse of the two, and involves too little of the positive and too much of the negative aspect of the task, such as a person who can't trust others. A maladaptation is not quite as bad and involves too much of the positive and too little of the negative, such as a person who trusts too much.

Children and adults

Perhaps Erikson's greatest innovation was to postulate not five stages, as Freud had done, but eight. Erikson elaborated Freud's genital stage into adolescence plus three stages of adulthood. We certainly don't stop developing -- especially psychologically -- after our twelfth or thirteenth birthdays; It seems only right to extend any theory of stages to cover later development!

Erikson also had some things to say about the interaction of generations, which he called mutuality. Freud had made it abundantly clear that a child's parents influence his or her development dramatically. Erikson pointed out that children influence their parents' development as well. The arrival of children, for example, into a couple's life, changes that life considerably, and moves the new parents along their developmental paths. It is even appropriate to add a third (and in some cases, a fourth) generation to the picture: Many of us have been influenced by our grandparents, and they by us.

A particularly clear example of mutuality can be seen in the problems of the teenage mother. Although the mother and her child may have a fine life together, often the mother is still involved in the tasks of adolescence, that is, in finding out who she is and how she fits into the larger society. The relationship she has or had with the child's father may have been immature on one or both sides, and if they don't marry, she will have to deal with the problems of finding and developing a relationship as well. The infant, on the other hand, has the simple, straight-forward needs that infants have, and the most important of these is a mother with the mature abilities and social support a mother should have. If the mother's parents step in to help, as one would expect, then they, too, are thrown off of their developmental tracks, back into a life-style they thought they had passed, and which they might find terribly demanding. And so on....

The first stage

The first stage, infancy or the oral-sensory stage, is approximately the first year or year and a half of life. The task is to develop trust without completely eliminating the capacity for mistrust.

If mom and dad can give the newborn a degree of familiarity, consistency, and continuity, then the child will develop the feeling that the world -- especially the social world -- is a safe place to be, that people are reliable and loving. Through the parents' responses, the child also learns to trust his or her own body and the biological urges that go with it.

If the parents are unreliable and inadequate, if they reject the infant or harm it, if other interests cause both parents to turn away from the infants needs to satisfy their own instead, then the infant will develop mistrust. He or she will be apprehensive and suspicious around people.

Please understand that this doesn't mean that the parents have to be perfect. In fact, parents who are overly protective of the child, are there the minute the first cry comes out, will lead that child into the maladaptive tendency Erikson calls sensory maladjustment: Overly trusting, even gullible, this person cannot believe anyone would mean them harm, and will use all the defenses at their command to retain their pollyanna perspective.

Worse, of course, is the child whose balance is tipped way over on the mistrust side: They will develop the malignant tendency of withdrawal, characterized by depression, paranoia, and possibly psychosis.

If the proper balance is achieved, the child will develop the virtue hope, the strong belief that, even when things are not going well, they will work out well in the end. One of the signs that a child is doing well in the first stage is when the child isn't overly upset by the need to wait a moment for the satisfaction of his or her needs: Mom or dad don't have to be perfect; I trust them enough to believe that, if they can't be here immediately, they will be here soon; Things may be tough now, but they will work out. This is the same ability that, in later life, gets us through disappointments in love, our careers, and many other domains of life.

Stage two

The second stage is the anal-muscular stage of early childhood, from about eighteen months to three or four years old. The task is to achieve a degree of autonomy while minimizing shame and doubt.

If mom and dad (and the other care-takers that often come into the picture at this point) permit the child, now a toddler, to explore and manipulate his or her environment, the child will develop a sense of autonomy or independence. The parents should not discourage the child, but neither should they push. A balance is required. People often advise new parents to be "firm but tolerant" at this stage, and the advice is good. This way, the child will develop both self-control and self-esteem.

On the other hand, it is rather easy for the child to develop instead a sense of shame and doubt. If the parents come down hard on any attempt to explore and be independent, the child will soon give up with the assumption that cannot and should not act on their own. We should keep in mind that even something as innocent as laughting at the toddler's efforts can lead the child to feel deeply ashamed, and to doubt his or her abilities.

And there are other ways to lead children to shame and doubt: If you give children unrestricted freedom and no sense of limits, or if you try to help children do what they should learn to do for themselves, you will also give them the impression that they are not good for much. If you aren't patient enough to wait for your child to tie his or her shoe-laces, your child will never learn to tie them, and will assume that this is too difficult to learn!

Nevertheless, a little "shame and doubt" is not only inevitable, but beneficial. Without it, you will develop the maladaptive tendency Erikson calls impulsiveness, a sort of shameless willfulness that leads you, in later childhood and even adulthood, to jump into things without proper consideration of your abilities.

Worse, of course, is too much shame and doubt, which leads to the malignancy Erikson calls compulsiveness. The compulsive person feels as if their entire being rides on everything they do, and so everything must be done perfectly. Following all the rules precisely keeps you from mistakes, and mistakes must be avoided at all costs. Many of you know how it feels to always be ashamed and always doubt yourself. A little more patience and tolerance with your own children may help them avoid your path. And give yourself a little slack, too!

If you get the proper, positive balance of autonomy and shame and doubt, you will develop the virtue of willpower or determination. One of the most admirable -- and frustrating -- thing about two- and three-year-olds is their determination. "Can do" is their motto. If we can preserve that "can do" attitude (with appropriate modesty to balance it) we are much better off as adults.

Stage three

Stage three is the genital-locomotor stage or play age. From three or four to five or six, the task confronting every child is to learn initiative without too much guilt.

Initiative means a positive response to the world's challenges, taking on responsibilities, learning new skills, feeling purposeful. Parents can encourage initiative by encouraging children to try out their ideas. We should accept and encourage fantasy and curiosity and imagination. This is a time for play, not for formal education. The child is now capable, as never before, of imagining a future situation, one that isn't a reality right now. Initiative is the attempt to make that non-reality a reality.

But if children can imagine the future, if they can plan, then they can be responsible as well, and guilty. If my two-year-old flushes my watch down the toilet, I can safely assume that there were no "evil intentions." It was just a matter of a shiny object going round and round and down. What fun! But if my five year old does the same thing... well, she should know what's going to happen to the watch, what's going to happen to daddy's temper, and what's going to happen to her! She can be guilty of the act, and she can begin to feel guilty as well. The capacity for moral judgement has arrived.

Erikson is, of course, a Freudian, and as such, he includes the Oedipal experience in this stage. From his perspective, the Oedipal crisis involves the reluctance a child feels in relinquishing his or her closeness to the opposite sex parent. A parent has the responsibility, socially, to enourage the child to "grow up -- you're not a baby anymore!" But if this process is done too harshly and too abruptly, the child learns to feel guilty about his or her feelings.

Too much initiative and too little guilt means a maladaptive tendency Erikson calls ruthlessness. The ruthless person takes the initiative alright; They have their plans, whether it's a matter of school or romance or politics or career. It's just that they don't care who they step on to achieve their goals. The goals are everything, and guilty feelings are for the weak. The extreme form of ruthlessess is sociopathy.

Ruthlessness is bad for others, but actually relatively easy on the ruthless person. Harder on the person is the malignancy of too much guilt, which Erikson calls inhibition. The inhibited person will not try things because "nothing ventured, nothing lost" and, particularly, nothing to feel guilty about. On the sexual, Oedipal, side, the inhibited person may be impotent or frigid.

A good balance leads to the psychosocial strength of purpose. A sense of purpose is something many people crave in their lives, yet many do not realize that they themselves make their purposes, through imagination and initiative. I think an even better word for this virtue would have been courage, the capacity for action despite a clear understanding of your limitations and past failings.

Stage four

Stage four is the latency stage, or the school-age child from about six to twelve. The task is to develop a capacity for industry while avoiding an excessive sense of inferiority. Children must "tame the imagination" and dedicate themselves to education and to learning the social skills their society requires of them.

There is a much broader social sphere at work now: The parents and other family members are joined by teachers and peers and other members of he community at large. They all contribute: Parents must encourage, teachers must care, peers must accept. Children must learn that there is pleasure not only in conceiving a plan, but in carrying it out. They must learn the feeling of success, whether it is in school or on the playground, academic or social.

A good way to tell the difference between a child in the third stage and one in the fourth stage is to look at the way they play games. Four-year-olds may love games, but they will have only a vague understanding of the rules, may change them several times during the course of the game, and be very unlikely to actually finish the game, unless it is by throwing the pieces at their opponents. A seven-year-old, on the other hand, is dedicated to the rules, considers them pretty much sacred, and is more likely to get upset if the game is not allowed to come to its required conclusion.

If the child is allowed too little success, because of harsh teachers or rejecting peers, for example, then he or she will develop instead a sense of inferiority or incompetence. An additional source of inferiority Erikson mentions is racism, sexism, and other forms of discrimination: If a child believes that success is related to who you are rather than to how hard you try, then why try?

Too much industry leads to the maladaptive tendency called narrow virtuosity. We see this in children who aren't allowed to "be children," the ones that parents or teachers push into one area of competence, without allowing the development of broader interests. These are the kids without a life: child actors, child athletes, child musicians, child prodigies of all sorts. We all admire their industry, but if we look a little closer, it's all that stands in the way of an empty life.

Much more common is the malignancy called inertia. This includes all of us who suffer from the "inferiority complexes" Alfred Adler talked about. If at first you don't succeed, don't ever try again! Many of us didn't do well in mathematics, for example, so we'd die before we took another math class. Others were humiliated instead in the gym class, so we never try out for a sport or play a game of raquetball. Others never developed social skills -- the most important skills of all -- and so we never go out in public. We become inert.

A happier thing is to develop the right balance of industry and inferiority -- that is, mostly industry with just a touch of inferiority to keep us sensibly humble. Then we have the virtue called competency.

Stage five

Stage five is adolescence, beginning with puberty and ending around 18 or 20 years old. The task during adolescence is to achieve ego identity and avoid role confusion. It was adolescence that interested Erikson first and most, and the patterns he saw here were the bases for his thinking about all the other stages.

Ego identity means knowing who you are and how you fit in to the rest of society. It requires that you take all you've learned about life and yourself and mold it into a unified self-image, one that your community finds meaningful.

There are a number of things that make things easier: First, we should have a mainstream adult culture that is worthy of the adolescent's respect, one with good adult role models and open lines of communication.

Further, society should provide clear rites of passage, certain accomplishments and rituals that help to distinguish the adult from the child. In primitive and traditional societies, an adolescent boy may be asked to leave the village for a period of time to live on his own, hunt some symbolic animal, or seek an inspirational vision. Boys and girls may be required to go through certain tests of endurance, symbolic ceremonies, or educational events. In one way or another, the distinction between the powerless, but irresponsible, time of childhood and the powerful and responsbile time of adulthood, is made clear.

Without these things, we are likely to see role confusion, meaning an uncertainty about one's place in society and the world. When an adolescent is confronted by role confusion, Erikson say he or she is suffering from an identity crisis. In fact, a common question adolescents in our society ask is a straight-forward question of identity: "Who am I?"

One of Erikson's suggestions for adolescence in our society is the psychosocial moratorium. He suggests you take a little "time out." If you have money, go to Europe. If you don't, bum around the U.S. Quit school and get a job. Quit your job and go to school. Take a break, smell the roses, get to know yourself. We tend to want to get to "success" as fast as possible, and yet few of us have ever taken the time to figure out what success means to us. A little like the young Oglala Lakota, perhaps we need to dream a little.

There is such a thing as too much "ego identity," where a person is so involved in a particular role in a particular society or subculture that there is no room left for tolerance. Erikson calls this maladaptive tendency fanaticism. A fanatic believes that his way is the only way. Adolescents are, of course, known for their idealism, and for their tendency to see things in black-and-white. These people will gather others around them and promote their beliefs and life-styles without regard to others' rights to disagree.

The lack of identity is perhaps more difficult still, and Erikson refers to the malignant tendency here as repudiation. They repudiate their membership in the world of adults and, even more, they repudiate their need for an identity. Some adolescents allow themselves to "fuse" with a group, especially the kind of group that is particularly eager to provide the details of your identity: religious cults, militaristic organizations, groups founded on hatred, groups that have divorced themselves from the painful demands of mainstream society. They may become involved in destructive activities, drugs, or alcohol, or you may withdraw into their own psychotic fantasies. After all, being "bad" or being "nobody" is better than not knowing who you are!

If you successfully negotiate this stage, you will have the virtue Erikson called fidelity. Fidelity means loyalty, the ability to live by societies standards despite their imperfections and incompleteness and inconsistencies. We are not talking about blind loyalty, and we are not talking about accepting the imperfections. After all, if you love your community, you will want to see it become the best it can be. But fidelity means that you have found a place in that community, a place that will allow you to contribute.

Stage six

If you have made it this far, you are in the stage of young adulthood, which lasts from about 18 to about 30. The ages in the adult stages are much fuzzier than in the childhood stages, and people may differ dramatically. The task is to achieve some degree of intimacy, as opposed to remaining in isolation.

Intimacy is the ability to be close to others, as a lover, a friend, and as a participant in society. Because you have a clear sense of who you are, you no longer need to fear "losing" yourself, as many adolescents do. The "fear of commitment" some people seem to exhibit is an example of immaturity in this stage. This fear isn't always so obvious. Many people today are always putting off the progress of their relationships: I'll get married (or have a family, or get involved in important social issues) as soon as I finish school, as soon as I have a job, as soon as I have a house, as soon as.... If you've been engaged for the last ten years, what's holding you back?

Neither should the young adult need to prove him- or herself anymore. A teenage relationship is often a matter of trying to establish identity through "couple-hood." Who am I? I'm her boy-friend. The young adult relationship should be a matter of two independent egos wanting to create something larger than themselves. We intuitively recognize this when we frown on a relationship between a young adult and a teenager: We see the potential for manipulation of the younger member of the party by the older.

Our society hasn't done much for young adults, either. The emphasis on careers, the isolation of urban living, the splitting apart of relationships because of our need for mobility, and the general impersonal nature of modern life prevent people from naturally developing their intimate relationships. I am typical of many people in having moved dozens of times in my life. I haven't the faintest idea what has happened to the kids I grew up with, or even my college buddies. My oldest friend lives a thousand miles away. I live where I do out of career necessity and, until recently, have felt no real sense of community.

Before I get too depressing, let me mention that many of you may not have had these experiences. If you grew up and stayed in your community, and especially if your community is a rural one, you are much more likely to have deep, long-lasting friendships, to have married your high school sweetheart, and to feel a great love for your community. But this style of life is quickly becoming an anachronism.

Erikson calls the maladaptive form promiscuity, refering particularly to the tendency to become intimate too freely, too easily, and without any depth to your intimacy. This can be true of your relationships with friends and neighbors and your whole community as well as with lovers.

The malignancy he calls exclusion, which refers to the tendency to isolate oneself from love, friendship, and community, and to develop a certain hatefulness in compensation for one's loneliness.

If you successfully negotiate this stage, you will instead carry with you for the rest of your life the virtue or psychosocial strength Erikson calls love. Love, in the context of his theory, means being able to put aside differences and antagonisms through "mutuality of devotion." It includes not only the love we find in a good marriage, but the love between friends and the love of one's neighbor, co-worker, and compatriot as well.

Stage seven

The seventh stage is that of middle adulthood. It is hard to pin a time to it, but it would include the period during which we are actively involved in raising children. For most people in our society, this would put it somewhere between the middle

48

twenties and the late fifties. The task here is to cultivate the proper balance of generativity and stagnation.

Generativity is an extension of love into the future. It is a concern for the next generation and all future generations. As such, it is considerably less "selfish" than the intimacy of the previous stage: Intimacy, the love between lovers or friends, is a love between equals, and it is necessarily reciprocal. Oh, of course we love each other unselfishly, but the reality is such that, if the love is not returned, we don't consider it a true love. With generativity, that implicit expectation of reciprocity isn't there, at least not as strongly. Few parents expect a "return on their investment" from their children; If they do, we don't think of them as very good parents!

Although the majority of people practice generativity by having and raising children, there are many other ways as well. Erikson considers teaching, writing, invention, the arts and sciences, social activism, and generally contributing to the welfare of future generations to be generativity as well -- anything, in fact, that satisfies that old "need to be needed."

Stagnation, on the other hand, is self-absorption, caring for no-one. The stagnant person ceases to be a productive member of society. It is perhaps hard to imagine that we should have any "stagnation" in our lives, but the maladaptive tendency Erikson calls overextension illustrates the problem: Some people try to be so generative that they no longer allow time for themselves, for rest and relaxation. The person who is overextended no longer contributes well. I'm sure we all know someone who belongs to so many clubs, or is devoted to so many causes, or tries to take so many classes or hold so many jobs that they no longer have time for any of them!

More obvious, of course, is the malignant tendency of rejectivity. Too little generativity and too much stagnation and you are no longer participating in or contributing to society. And much of what we call "the meaning of life" is a matter of how we participate and what we contribute.

This is the stage of the "midlife crisis." Sometimes men and women take a look at their lives and ask that big, bad question "what am I doing all this for?" Notice the question carefully: Because their focus is on themselves, they ask what, rather than whom, they are doing it for. In their panic at getting older and not having experienced or accomplished what they imagined they would when they were younger, they try to recapture their youth. Men are often the most flambouyant examples: They leave their long-suffering wives, quit their humdrum jobs, buy some "hip" new clothes, and start hanging around singles bars. Of course, they seldom find what they are looking for, because they are looking for the wrong thing!

But if you are successful at this stage, you will have a capacity for caring that will serve you through the rest of your life.

Stage eight

This last stage, referred to delicately as late adulthood or maturity, or less delicately as old age, begins sometime around retirement, after the kids have gone, say somewhere around 60. Some older folks will protest and say it only starts when you feel old and so on, but that's an effect of our youth-worshipping culture, which has even old people avoiding any acknowledgement of age. In Erikson's theory, reaching this stage is a good thing, and not reaching it suggests that earlier problems retarded your development!

The task is to develop ego integrity with a minimal amount of despair. This stage, especially from the perspective of youth, seems like the most difficult of all. First comes a detachment from society, from a sense of usefulness, for most people in our culture. Some retire from jobs they've held for years; others find their duties as parents coming to a close; most find that their input is no longer requested or required.

Then there is a sense of biological uselessness, as the body no longer does everything it used to. Women go through a sometimes dramatic menopause; Men often find they can no longer "rise to the occasion." Then there are the illnesses of old age, such as arthritis, diabetes, heart problems, concerns about breast and ovarian and prostrate cancers. There come fears about things that one was never afraid of before -- the flu, for example, or just falling down.

Along with the illnesses come concerns of death. Friends die. Relatives die. One's spouse dies. It is, of course, certain that you, too, will have your turn. Faced with all this, it might seem like everyone would feel despair.

In response to this despair, some older people become preoccupied with the past. After all, that's where things were better. Some become preoccupied with their failures, the bad decisions they made, and regret that (unlike some in the previous stage) they really don't have the time or energy to reverse them. We find some older people become depressed, spiteful, paranoid, hypochondriacal, or developing the patterns of senility with or without physical bases.

Ego integrity means coming to terms with your life, and thereby coming to terms with the end of life. If you are able to look back and accept the course of events, the choices made, your life as you lived it, as being necessary, then you needn't fear death. Although most of you are not at this point in life, perhaps you can still sympathize by considering your life up to now. We've all made mistakes, some of them pretty nasty ones; Yet, if you hadn't made these mistakes, you wouldn't be who you are. If you had been very fortunate, or if you had played it safe and made very few mistakes, your life would not have been as rich as is.

The maladaptive tendency in stage eight is called presumption. This is what happens when a person "presumes" ego integrity without actually facing the difficulties of old age. The malignant tendency is called disdain, by which Erikson means a contempt of life, one's own or anyone's.

Someone who approaches death without fear has the strength Erikson calls wisdom. He calls it a gift to children, because "healthy children will not fear life if their elders have integrity enough not to fear death." He suggests that a person must be somewhat gifted to be truly wise, but I would like to suggest that you understand "gifted" in as broad a fashion as possible: I have found that there are people of very modest gifts who have taught me a great deal, not by their wise words, but by their simple and gentle approach to life and death, by their "generosity of spirit."

The Diagnostic and Statistical Manual of Mental Disorders (DSM) is published by the American Psychiatric Association and provides a common language and standard criteria for the classification of mental disorders. It is used in the United States and in varying degrees around the world, by clinicians, researchers, psychiatric drug regulation agencies, health insurance companies, pharmaceutical companies, and policy makers. The DSM has attracted controversy and criticism as well as praise. There have been five revisions since it was first published in 1952, gradually including more mental disorders, although some have been removed and are no longer considered to be mental disorders, most notably homosexuality.

The manual evolved from systems for collecting census and psychiatric hospital statistics, and from a manual developed by the US Army, and was dramatically revised in 1980. The last major revision was the fourth edition ("DSM-IV"), published in 1994, although a "text revision" was produced in 2000. The fifth edition ("DSM-5") is currently in consultation, planning and preparation, due for publication in May 2013.

ICD-10 Chapter V: Mental and behavioural disorders, part of the International Classification of Diseases produced by the World Health Organization (WHO), is another commonly used guide, more so in Europe and other parts of the world. The coding system used in the DSM-IV is designed to correspond with the codes used in the ICD, although not all codes may match at all times because the two publications are not revised synchronously.

Uses

Many mental health professionals use the manual to determine and help communicate a patient's diagnosis after an evaluation; hospitals, clinics, and insurance companies in the US also generally require a 'five axis' DSM diagnosis of all the patients treated. The DSM can be used clinically in this way, and also to categorize patients using diagnostic criteria for research purposes. Studies done on specific disorders often recruit patients whose symptoms match the criteria listed in the DSM for that disorder. An international survey of psychiatrists in 66 countries comparing use of the

ICD-10 and DSM-IV found the former was more often used for clinical diagnosis while the latter was more valued for research.

The DSM, including DSM-IV, is a registered trademark belonging to the American Psychiatric Association (APA). It is a bestselling publication from which APA makes "huge profits" and gains considerable clout in world psychiatry, especially as many reputed research journals require studies to use DSM classification in order to be published.

History

The initial impetus for developing a classification of mental disorders in the United States was the need to collect statistical information. The first official attempt was the 1840 census which used a single category, "idiocy/insanity". In 1917, a "Committee on Statistics" from what is now known as the American Psychiatric Association (APA), together with the National Commission on Mental Hygiene, developed a new guide for mental hospitals called the "Statistical Manual for the Use of Institutions for the Insane", which included 22 diagnoses. This was subsequently revised several times by APA over the years. APA, along with the New York Academy of Medicine, also provided the psychiatric nomenclature subsection of the US medical guide, the "Standard Classified Nomenclature of Disease", referred to as the "Standard".

DSM-I (1952)

World War II saw the large-scale involvement of US psychiatrists in the selection, processing, assessment and treatment of soldiers. This moved the focus away from mental institutions and traditional clinical perspectives. A committee that was headed by psychiatrist Brigadier General William C. Menninger developed a new classification scheme called Medical 203 that was issued in 1943 as a "War Department Technical Bulletin" under the auspices of the Office of the Surgeon General. The foreword to the DSM-I states the US Navy had itself made some minor revisions but "the Army established a much more sweeping revision, abandoning the basic outline of the Standard and attempting to express present day concepts of mental disturbance. This nomenclature eventually was adopted by all Armed Forces", and "assorted modifications of the Armed Forces nomenclature [were] introduced into many clinics and hospitals by psychiatrists returning from military duty." The Veterans Administration also adopted a slightly modified version of Medical 203.

In 1949, the World Health Organization published the sixth revision of the International Statistical Classification of Diseases (ICD) which included a section on mental disorders for the first time. The foreword to DSM-1 states this "categorized mental disorders in rubrics similar to those of the Armed Forces nomenclature." An APA Committee on Nomenclature and Statistics was empowered to develop a version specifically for use in the United States, to standardize the diverse and confused usage of different documents. In 1950 the APA committee undertook a review and consultation. It circulated an adaptation of Medical 203, the VA system and the Standard's Nomenclature, to approximately 10% of APA members. 46% replied, of which 93% approved, and after some further revisions (resulting in it being called DSM-I), the Diagnostic and Statistical Manual of Mental Disorders was approved in 1951 and published in 1952. The structure and conceptual framework were the same as in Medical 203, and many passages of text identical. The manual was 130 pages long and listed 106 mental disorders.

DSM-II (1968)

Although the APA was closely involved in the next significant revision of the mental disorder section of the ICD (version 8 in 1968), it decided to also go ahead with a revision of the DSM. It was also published in 1968, listed 182 disorders, and was 134 pages long. It was quite similar to the DSM-I. The term "reaction" was dropped but the term "neurosis" was retained. Both the DSM-I and the DSM-II reflected the predominant psychodynamic psychiatry, although they also included biological perspectives and concepts from Kraepelin's system of classification. Symptoms were not specified in detail for specific disorders. Many were seen as reflections of broad underlying conflicts or maladaptive reactions to life problems, rooted in a distinction between neurosis and psychosis (roughly, anxiety/depression broadly in touch with reality, or hallucinations/delusions appearing disconnected from reality). Sociological and biological knowledge was also incorporated, in a model that did not emphasize a clear boundary between normality and abnormality.

Following controversy and protests from gay activists at APA annual conferences from 1970 to 1973, as well as the emergence of new data from researchers such as Alfred Kinsey and Evelyn Hooker, the seventh printing of the DSM-II, in 1974, no longer listed homosexuality as a category of disorder. But through the efforts of psychiatrist Robert Spitzer, who had led the DSM-II development committee, a vote by the APA trustees in 1973, and confirmed by the wider APA membership in 1974, the diagnosis was replaced with the category of "sexual orientation disturbance".

DSM-III (1980)

In 1974, the decision to create a new revision of the DSM was made, and Robert Spitzer was selected as chairman of the task force. The initial impetus was to make the DSM nomenclature consistent with the International Statistical Classification of Diseases and Related Health Problems (ICD), published by the World Health Organization. The revision took on a far wider mandate under the influence and control of Spitzer and his chosen committee members. One goal was to improve the uniformity and validity of psychiatric diagnosis in the wake of a number of critiques, including the famous Rosenhan experiment. There was also a need to standardize diagnostic practices within the US and with other countries after research showed that psychiatric diagnoses differed markedly between Europe and the USA. The establishment of these criteria was also an attempt to facilitate the pharmaceutical regulatory process.

The criteria adopted for many of the mental disorders were taken from the Research Diagnostic Criteria (RDC) and Feighner Criteria, which had just been developed by a group of research-orientated psychiatrists based primarily at Washington University in St. Louis and the New York State Psychiatric Institute. Other criteria, and potential new categories of disorder, were established by consensus during meetings of the committee, as chaired by Spitzer. A key aim was to base categorization on colloquial English descriptive language (which would be easier to use by Federal administrative offices), rather than assumptions of etiology, although its categorical approach assumed each particular pattern of symptoms in a category reflected a particular underlying pathology (an approach described as "neo-Kraepelinian"). The psychodynamic or physiologic view was abandoned, in favor of a regulatory or legislative model. A new "multiaxial" system attempted to yield a picture more amenable to a statistical population census, rather than just a simple diagnosis. Spitzer argued, "mental disorders are a subset of medical disorders" but the task force decided on the DSM statement: "Each of the mental disorders is conceptualized as a clinically significant behavioral or psychological syndrome."

The first draft of the DSM-III was prepared within a year. Many new categories of disorder were introduced; a number of the unpublished documents that aim to justify them have recently come to light. Field trials sponsored by the U.S. National Institute of Mental Health (NIMH) were conducted between 1977 and 1979 to test the reliability of the new diagnoses. A controversy emerged regarding deletion of the concept of neurosis, a mainstream of psychoanalytic theory and therapy but seen as vague and unscientific by the DSM task force. Faced with enormous political opposition, so the DSM-III was in serious danger of not being approved by the APA Board of Trustees unless "neurosis" was included in some capacity, a political compromise reinserted the term in parentheses after the word "disorder" in some cases. Additionally, the diagnosis of ego-dystonic homosexuality replaced the DSM-II category of "sexual orientation disturbance".

Finally published in 1980, the DSM-III was 494 pages long and listed 265 diagnostic categories. It rapidly came into widespread international use by multiple stakeholders and has been termed a revolution or transformation in psychiatry. However Robert Spitzer later criticized his own work on it in an interview with Adam Curtis saying it led to the medicalization of 20-30 percent of the population who may not have had any serious mental problems.

DSM-III-R (1987)

In 1987 the DSM-III-R was published as a revision of DSM-III, under the direction of Spitzer. Categories were renamed, reorganized, and significant changes in criteria were made. Six categories were deleted while others were added. Controversial diagnoses such as pre-menstrual dysphoric disorder and Masochistic Personality Disorder were considered and discarded. "Sexual orientation disturbance" was also removed, but was largely subsumed under "sexual disorder not otherwise specified" which can include "persistent and marked distress about one's sexual orientation." Altogether, DSM-III-R contained 292 diagnoses and was 567 pages long.

DSM-IV (1994)

In 1994, DSM-IV was published, listing 297 disorders in 886 pages. The task force was chaired by Allen Frances. A steering committee of 27 people was introduced, including four psychologists. The steering committee created 13 work groups of 5–16 members. Each work group had approximately 20 advisers. The work groups conducted a three step process. First, each group conducted an extensive literature review of their diagnoses. Then they requested data from researchers, conducting analyses to determine which criteria required change, with instructions to be conservative. Finally, they conducted multicenter field trials relating diagnoses to clinical practice. A major change from previous versions was the inclusion of a clinical significance criterion to almost half of all the categories, which required symptoms cause "clinically significant distress or impairment in social, occupational, or other important areas of functioning".

DSM-IV-TR (2000)

A "Text Revision" of the DSM-IV, known as the DSM-IV-TR, was published in 2000. The diagnostic categories and the vast majority of the specific criteria for diagnosis were unchanged. The text sections giving extra information on each diagnosis were updated, as were some of the diagnostic codes in order to maintain consistency with the ICD.

DSM-IV-TR: the current version

Categorization

The DSM-IV is a categorical classification system. The categories are prototypes, and a patient with a close approximation to the prototype is said to have that disorder.

DSM-IV states, "there is no assumption each category of mental disorder is a completely discrete entity with absolute boundaries..." but isolated, low-grade and no criterion (unlisted for a given disorder) symptoms are not given importance. Qualifiers are sometimes used, for example mild, moderate or severe forms of a disorder. For nearly half the disorders, symptoms must be sufficient to cause "clinically significant distress or impairment in social, occupational, or other important areas of functioning", although DSM-IV-TR removed the distress criterion from tic disorders and several of the paraphilias. Each category of disorder has a numeric code taken from the ICD coding system, used for health service (including insurance) administrative purposes.

Multi-axial system

The DSM-IV organizes each psychiatric diagnosis into five dimensions (axes) relating to different aspects of disorder or disability:

- *Axis I:* Clinical disorders, including major mental disorders, and learning disorders
- *Axis II:* Personality disorders and intellectual disabilities (although developmental disorders, such as Autism, were coded on Axis II in the previous edition, these disorders are now included on Axis I)
- *Axis III:* Acute medical conditions and physical disorders
- *Axis IV:* Psychosocial and environmental factors contributing to the disorder
- *Axis V:* Global Assessment of Functioning or Children's Global Assessment Scale for children and teens under the age of 18

Common Axis I disorders include depression, anxiety disorders, bipolar disorder, ADHD, autism spectrum disorders, anorexia nervosa, bulimia nervosa, and schizophrenia.

Common Axis II disorders include personality disorders: paranoid personality disorder, schizoid personality disorder, schizotypal personality disorder, borderline personality disorder, antisocial personality disorder, narcissistic personality disorder, histrionic personality disorder, avoidant personality disorder, dependent personality disorder, obsessive-compulsive personality disorder, and intellectual disabilities.

Common Axis III disorders include brain injuries and other medical/physical disorders which may aggravate existing diseases or present symptoms similar to other disorders.

Cautions

The DSM-IV-TR states, because it is produced for the completion of federal legislative mandates, its use by people without clinical training can lead to inappropriate application of its contents. Appropriate use of the diagnostic criteria is said to require extensive clinical training, and its contents "cannot simply be applied in a cookbook fashion". The APA notes diagnostic labels are primarily for use as a "convenient shorthand" among professionals. The DSM advises laypersons should consult the DSM only to obtain information, not to make diagnoses, and people who may have a mental disorder should be referred to psychological counseling or treatment. Further, a shared diagnosis or label may have different causes or require different treatments; for this reason the DSM contains no information regarding treatment or cause. The range of the DSM represents an extensive scope of psychiatric and psychological issues or conditions, and it is not exclusive to what may be considered "illnesses".

Criticism

Validity and reliability

The most fundamental scientific criticism of the DSM concerns the validity and reliability of its diagnoses. This refers, roughly, to whether the disorders it defines are actually real conditions in people in the real world, that can be consistently identified by its criteria. These are long-standing criticisms of the DSM, originally highlighted by the Rosenhan experiment in the 1970s, and continuing despite some improved reliability since the introduction of more specific rule-based criteria for each condition.

Proponents argue that the inter-rater reliability of DSM diagnoses (via a specialized Structured Clinical Interview for DSM-IV (SCID) rather than usual psychiatric assessment) is reasonable, and that there is good evidence of distinct patterns of mental, behavioral or neurological dysfunction to which the DSM disorders correspond well. It is accepted, however, that there is an "enormous" range of reliability findings in studies, and that validity is unclear because, given the lack of diagnostic laboratory or neuroimaging tests, standard clinical interviews are "inherently limited" and only a ("flawed") "best estimate diagnosis" is possible even with full assessment of all data over time.

Critics, such as psychiatrist Niall McLaren, argue that the DSM lacks validity because it has no relation to an agreed scientific model of mental disorder and therefore the decisions taken about its categories (or even the question of categories vs. dimensions) were not scientific ones; and that it lacks reliability partly because different diagnoses share many criteria, and what appear to be different criteria are often just rewordings of the same idea, meaning that the decision to allocate one diagnosis or another to a patient is to some extent a matter of personal prejudice.

Superficial symptoms

By design, the DSM is primarily concerned with the signs and symptoms of mental disorders, rather than the underlying causes. It claims to collect them together based on statistical or clinical patterns. As such, it has been compared to a naturalist's field guide to birds, with similar advantages and disadvantages. The lack of a causative or explanatory basis, however, is not specific to the DSM, but rather reflects a general lack of pathophysiological understanding of psychiatric disorders. As DSM-III chief architect Robert Spitzer and DSM-IV editor Michael First outlined in 2005, "little progress has been made toward understanding the pathophysiological processes and etiology of mental disorders. If anything, the research has shown the situation is even more complex than initially imagined, and we believe not enough is known to structure the classification of psychiatric disorders according to etiology." However, the DSM is based on an underlying structure that assumes discrete medical disorders that can be separated from each other by symptom patterns. Its claim to be "atheoretical" is held to be unconvincing because it makes sense if and only if all mental disorder is categorical by nature, which only a biological model of mental disorder can satisfy. However, the Manual recognizes psychological causes of mental disorder, e.g. PTSD, so that it negates its only possible justification.

The DSM's focus on superficial symptoms is claimed to be largely a result of necessity (assuming such a manual is nevertheless produced), since there is no agreement on a more explanatory classification system. Reviewers note, however, that this approach is undermining research, including in genetics, because it results in the grouping of individuals who have very little in common except superficial criteria as per DSM or ICD diagnosis.

Despite the lack of consensus on underlying causation, advocates for specific psychopathological paradigms have nonetheless faulted the current diagnostic scheme for not incorporating evidence-based models or findings from other areas of science. A recent example is evolutionary psychologists' criticism that the DSM does not differentiate between genuine cognitive malfunctions and those induced by psychological adaptations, a key distinction within evolutionary psychology, but one widely challenged within general psychology.[34][35][36] Another example is a strong operationalist viewpoint, which contends that reliance on operational definitions, as purported by the DSM, necessitates that intuitive concepts such as depression be replaced by specific measurable concepts before they are scientifically meaningful. One critic states of psychologists that "Instead of replacing 'metaphysical' terms such as 'desire' and 'purpose', they used it to legitimize them by giving them operational definitions...the initial, quite radical operationalist ideas eventually came to serve as little more than a 'reassurance fetish' (Koch 1992) for mainstream methodological practice."

Dividing lines

Despite caveats in the introduction to the DSM, it has long been argued that its system of classification makes unjustified categorical distinctions between disorders, and uses arbitrary cut-offs between normal and abnormal. A 2009 psychiatric review noted that attempts to demonstrate natural boundaries between related DSM syndromes, or between a common DSM syndrome and normality, have failed. Some argue that rather than a categorical approach, a fully dimensional, spectrum or complaint-oriented approach would better reflect the evidence.

In addition, it is argued that the current approach based on exceeding a threshold of symptoms does not adequately take into account the context in which a person is living, and to what extent there is internal disorder of an individual versus a psychological response to adverse situations. The DSM does include a step ("Axis IV") for outlining "Psychosocial and environmental factors contributing to the disorder" once someone is diagnosed with that particular disorder.

Because an individual's degree of impairment is often not correlated with symptom counts, and can stem from various individual and social factors, the DSM's standard of distress or disability can often produce false positives. On the other hand, individuals who don't meet symptom counts may nevertheless experience comparable distress or disability in their life.

Despite doubts about arbitrary cut-offs, yes/no decisions often need to be made (e.g. whether a person will be provided a treatment) and the rest of medicine is committed to categories, so it is thought unlikely that any formal national or international classification will adopt a fully dimensional format.

Cultural bias

Some psychiatrists also argue that current diagnostic standards rely on an exaggerated interpretation of neurophysiological findings and so understate the scientific importance of social-psychological variables. Advocating a more culturally sensitive approach to psychology, critics such as Carl Bell and Marcello Maviglia contend that the cultural and ethnic diversity of individuals is often discounted by researchers and service providers. In addition, current diagnostic guidelines have been criticized as having a fundamentally Euro-American outlook. Although these guidelines have been widely implemented, opponents argue that even when a diagnostic criteria set is accepted across different cultures, it does not necessarily indicate that the underlying constructs have any validity within those cultures; even reliable application can only demonstrate consistency, not legitimacy. Cross-cultural psychiatrist Arthur Kleinman contends that the Western bias is ironically illustrated in the introduction of cultural factors to the DSM-IV: the fact that disorders or concepts from non-Western or non-mainstream cultures are described as "culture-bound", whereas standard psychiatric diagnoses are given no cultural qualification whatsoever, is to Kleinman revelatory of an underlying assumption that Western cultural phenomena are universal. Kleinman's negative view towards the culture-bound syndrome is largely shared by other cross-cultural critics, common responses included both disappointment over the large number of documented non-Western mental disorders still left out, and frustration that even those included were often misinterpreted or misrepresented. Many mainstream psychiatrists have also been dissatisfied with these new culture-bound diagnoses, although not for the same reasons. Robert Spitzer, a lead architect of the DSM-III, has held the opinion that the addition of cultural formulations was an attempt to placate cultural critics, and that they lack any scientific motivation or support. Spitzer also posits that the new culture-bound diagnoses are rarely used in practice, maintaining that the standard diagnoses apply regardless of the culture involved. In general, the mainstream psychiatric opinion remains that if a diagnostic category is valid, cross-cultural factors are either irrelevant or are only significant to specific symptom presentations.

Drug companies and medicalization

It has also been alleged that the way the categories of the DSM are structured, as well as the substantial expansion of the number of categories, are representative of an increasing medicalization of human nature, which may be attributed to disease mongering by pharmaceutical companies and psychiatrists, whose influence has dramatically grown in recent decades. Of the authors who selected and defined the DSM-IV psychiatric disorders, roughly half had had financial relationships with the pharmaceutical industry at one time, raising the prospect of a direct conflict of interest. In 2005, then American Psychiatric Association President Steven Sharfstein released a statement in which he conceded that psychiatrists had "allowed the biopsychosocial model to become the bio-bio-bio model".

However, although the number of identified diagnoses has increased by more than 200% (from 106 in DSM-I to 365 in DSM-IV-TR), psychiatrists such as Zimmerman and Spitzer argue it almost entirely represents greater specification of the forms of pathology, thereby allowing better grouping of more similar patients.

Political controversies

There is scientific and political controversy regarding the continued inclusion of sex-related diagnoses such as the paraphilias (sexual fetishes) and hypoactive sexual desire disorder (low sex drive). Critics of these and other controversial diagnoses often cite the DSM's previous inclusion of homosexuality, and the APA's eventual decision to remove it, as a precedent for current disputes. A survey has suggested however that around the world a majority of psychiatrist view homosexuality as indicating a mental illness. Stanton Jones, Ph.D. and Mark Yarhouse, Psy.D challenge studies which have run tests on "a group of "healthy" homosexuals and compared those results with results from a group of heterosexuals." as being "the logical equivalent" to if a "sample of intellectually gifted women performed as well as a sample of men on a math test." Jones and Yarhouse agree however that such studies have proven "it is not the case that all homosexuals are manifestly disturbed." The consensus though from the American Psychiatric Association, American Psychological Association, and other institutions in other countries, is that the research and clinical literature demonstrate that same-sex sexual and romantic attractions, feelings, and behaviors are normal and positive variations of human sexuality. Leaders of the Hearing Voices Network such as psychiatrist Marius Romme have claimed that many people who hallucinate "are like homosexuals in the 1950s -- in need of liberation, not cure."

Disputes over inclusion or exclusion can underscore the fact that reevaluation of controversial disorders can be viewed as a political as well as scientific decision. Indeed, Robert Spitzer, a past editor and leading proponent of scientific impartiality in the DSM, conceded that a significant reason that certain diagnoses (the paraphilias) would not, in his opinion, be removed from the DSM is because "it would be a public relations disaster for psychiatry". A similar line of criticism has appeared in nonspecialist venues. In 1997, Harper's Magazine published an essay, ostensibly a book review of the DSM-IV, that criticized the lack of hard science and the proliferation of disorders. The language of the DSM was described as "simultaneously precise and vague" in order to provide an aura of scientific objectivity yet not limit psychiatrists in a semantic or financial sense, and the manual itself compared to "a militia's Web page, insofar as it constitutes an alternative reality under siege" by critics.

Consumers

A Consumer is a person who has accessed psychiatric services and been given a diagnosis from the *Diagnostic and Statistical Manual of Mental Disorders*. Some consumers are relieved to find that they have a recognized condition to which they can give a name. Indeed, many people self-diagnose. Others, however, feel they have been given a "label" that invites social stigma and discrimination, or one that they simply do not feel is accurate. Diagnoses can become internalized and affect an individual's self-identity, and some psychotherapists find that this can worsen symptoms and inhibit the healing process. Some in the Consumer/Survivor/Ex-Patient Movement actively campaign against their diagnosis, or its assumed implications, and/or against the DSM system in general. It has been noted that the DSM often uses definitions and terminology that are inconsistent with a recovery model, and that can erroneously imply excess psychopathology (e.g. multiple "comorbid" diagnoses) or chronicity.

DSM-5: the next version

The next (fifth) edition of the Diagnostic and Statistical Manual of Mental Disorders (DSM), DSM-5, is currently in consultation, planning and preparation. It is due for publication in May 2013. APA has a website about the development, including draft versions, of what it is now referring to as the DSM-5 (rather than the roman numeral). It includes several changes, including proposed deletion of several types of schizophrenia.

Phobia

A phobia (from the Greek: φόβος,*phóbos*, meaning "fear" or "morbid fear") is defined as a persistent fear of an object or situation in which the sufferer commits to great lengths in avoiding despite the fear, typically disproportional to the actual danger posed, often being recognized as irrational. In the event the phobia cannot be avoided entirely, the sufferer will endure the situation or object with marked distress and significant interference in social or occupational activities. The terms *distress* and *impairment* as defined by the Diagnostic and Statistical Manual of Mental Disorders, Fourth Edition (DSM-IV-TR) should also take into account the context of the sufferer's environment if attempting a diagnosis. The DSM-IV-TR states that if a phobic stimulus, whether it be an object or a social situation, is absent entirely in an environment - a diagnosis cannot be made. An example of this situation would be an individual who has a fear of mice (Suriphobia) but lives in an area devoid of mice. Even though the concept of mice causes marked distress and impairment within the individual, because the individual does not encounter mice in the environment no actual distress or impairment is ever experienced. Proximity and the degree to which escape from the phobic stimulus should also be considered. As the sufferer approaches a phobic stimulus, anxiety levels increase (e.g. as one gets closer to a snake, fear increases in Ophidiophobia), and the degree to which escape of the phobic stimulus is limited has the effect of varying the intensity of fear in instances such as riding an elevator (e.g. anxiety increases at the midway point between floors and decreases when the floor is reached and the doors open). Finally, a point warranting clarification is that the term phobia is an encompassing term and when discussed is usually done in terms of specific phobias and social phobias. Specific phobias are nouns such as arachnophobia or acrophobia which, as the name implies, are specific, and social phobia are phobias within social situations such as public speaking and crowded areas. The following article will be broken down into two sections: Specific Phobias and Social Phobias. Focal points that will be addressed are areas such as epidemiology, etiology, criteria for diagnosis etc.

Specific Phobias

As briefly mentioned above, a specific phobia is a marked and persistent fear of an object or situation which brings about an excessive or unreasonable fear when in the presence of, or anticipating, a specific object; furthermore, the specific phobias may also include concerns with losing control, panicking, and fainting which is the direct result of an encounter with the phobia. The important distinction from social phobias are specific phobias are defined in regards to objects or situations whereas social phobias emphasizes more on social fear and the evaluations that might accompany them.

Diagnosis

The diagnostic criteria for 300.29 Specific Phobias as outlined by the DSM-IV-TR:

1. Marked and persistent fear that is excessive or unreasonable, cued by the presence or anticipation of a specific object or situation (e.g., flying, heights, animals, receiving an injection, seeing blood).
2. Exposure to the phobic stimulus almost invariably provokes an immediate anxiety response, which may take the form of a situationally bound or situationally predisposed panic attack. Note: In children, the anxiety may be expressed by crying, tantrums, freezing, or clinging.
3. The person recognizes that the fear is excessive or unreasonable. Note: In children, this feature may be absent.
4. The phobic situation(s) is avoided or else is endured with intense anxiety or distress.
5. The avoidance, anxious anticipation or distress in the feared situation(s) interferes significantly with the person's normal routine, occupational (or academic) functioning, or social activities or relationships, or there is marked distress about having the phobia.
6. In individuals under age 18 years, the duration is at least 6 months.
7. The anxiety, panic attack, or phobic avoidance associated with the specific object or situation are not better accounted for by another mental disorder, such as Obsessive-Compulsive Disorder (e.g., fear of dirt in someone with an obsession about contamination), Posttraumatic Stress Disorder (e.g., avoidance of stimuli associated

with a severe stressor), Separation Anxiety Disorder (e.g., avoidance of school), Social Phobia (e.g., avoidance of social situations because of fear of embarrassment), Panic Disorder With Agoraphobia, or Agoraphobia Without History of Panic Disorder.

Etiology

Environmental

This is caused by what are called neutral, unconditioned, and conditioned stimuli, which trigger either conditioned or unconditioned responses. An example would be a person who was attacked by a dog (the unconditioned stimulus) would respond with an unconditioned response. When this happens, the unconditioned stimulus of them being attacked by the dog would become conditioned, and to this now conditioned stimulus, they would develop a conditioned response. If the occurrence had enough of an impact on this certain person then they would develop a fear of that dog, or in some cases, an irrational fear of all dogs.

Phobias are known as an emotional response learned because of difficult life experiences. Generally phobias occur when fear produced by a threatening situation is transmitted to other similar situations, while the original fear is often repressed or forgotten. The excessive, unreasoning fear of water, for example, may be based on a childhood experience of almost drowning. The individual attempts to avoid that situation in the future, a response that, while reducing anxiety in the short term, reinforces the association of the situation with the onset of anxiety.

Some phobias are generated from the observation of a parent's or sibling's reaction. The observer then can take in the information and generate a fear of whatever they experienced.

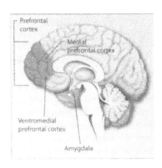

🔲

Regions of the brain associated with phobias

Neurobiology

Phobias are generally caused by an event recorded by the amygdala and hippocampus and labeled as deadly or dangerous; thus whenever a specific situation is approached again the body reacts as if the event were happening repeatedly afterward. Treatment comes in some way or another as a replacing of the memory and reaction to the previous event perceived as deadly with something more realistic and based more rationally. In reality most phobias are irrational, in that the subconscious association causes far more fear than is warranted based on the actual danger of the stimulus; a person with a phobia of water may admit that their physiological arousal is irrational and over-reactive, but this alone does not cure the phobia.

Phobias are more often than not linked to the amygdala, an area of the brain located behind the pituitary gland in the limbic system. The amygdala may trigger secretion of hormones that affect fear and aggression. When the fear or aggression response is initiated, the amygdala may trigger the release of hormones into the body to put the human body into an "alert" state, in which they are ready to move, run, fight, etc. This defensive "alert" state and response is generally referred to in psychology as the fight-or-flight response.

Clinical phobias

Psychologists and psychiatrists classify most phobias into three categories and, according to the Diagnostic and Statistical Manual of Mental Disorders, Fourth Edition (DSM-IV), such phobias are considered to be sub-types of anxiety disorder. The three categories are:

- Social phobia- fears involving other people or social situations such as performance anxiety or fears of embarrassment by scrutiny of others, such as eating in public. Overcoming social phobia is often very difficult without the help of therapy or support groups. Social phobia may be further subdivided into

  o   generalized social phobia (also known as social anxiety disorder or simply social anxiety) and

  o   specific social phobia, in which anxiety is triggered only in specific situations. The symptoms may extend to psychosomatic manifestation of physical problems. For example, sufferers of paruresis find it difficult or impossible to urinate in reduced levels of privacy. This goes far beyond mere preference: when the condition triggers, the person physically cannot empty their bladder.

- Specific phobias - fear of a single specific panic trigger such as spiders, snakes, dogs, water, heights, flying, catching a specific illness, etc. Many people have these fears but to a lesser degree than those who suffer from specific phobias. People with the phobias specifically avoid the entity they fear.

- Agoraphobia - a generalized fear of leaving home or a small familiar 'safe' area, and of possible panic attacks that might follow. May also be caused by various specific phobias such as fear of open spaces, social embarrassment (social agoraphobia), fear of contamination (fear of germs, possibly complicated by obsessive-compulsive disorder) or PTSD (post traumatic stress disorder) related to a trauma that occurred out of doors.

Phobias vary in severity among individuals. Some individuals can simply avoid the subject of their fear and suffer relatively mild anxiety over that fear. Others suffer full-fledged panic attacks with all the associated disabling symptoms. Most individuals understand that they are suffering from an irrational fear, but they are powerless to override their initial panic reaction.

Treatments

Various methods are claimed to treat phobias. Their proposed benefits may vary from person to person.

Some therapists use virtual reality or imagery exercise to desensitize patients to the feared entity. These are parts of systematic desensitization therapy.

Cognitive behavioral therapy (CBT) can be beneficial. Cognitive behavioral therapy lets the patient understand the cycle of negative thought patterns, and ways to change these thought patterns. CBT may be conducted in a group setting. Gradual desensitisation treatment and CBT are often successful, provided the patient is willing to endure some discomfort. In one clinical trial, 90% of patients were observed with no longer having a phobic reaction after successful CBT treatment.

Eye Movement Desensitization and Reprocessing (EMDR) has been demonstrated in peer-reviewed clinical trials to be effective in treating some phobias. Mainly used to treat Post-traumatic stress disorder, EMDR has been demonstrated as effective in easing phobia symptoms following a specific trauma, such as a fear of dogs following a dog bite.

Hypnotherapy coupled with Neuro-linguistic programming can also be used to help remove the associations that trigger a phobic reaction. However, lack of research and scientific testing compromises its status as an effective treatment.

Antidepressant medications such SSRIs, MAOIs may be helpful in some cases of phobia. Benzodiazepines may be useful in acute treatment of severe symptoms but the risk benefit ratio is against their long-term use in phobic disorders.

There are also new pharmacological approaches, which target learning and memory processes that occur during psychotherapy. For example, it has been shown that glucocorticoids can enhance extinction-based psychotherapy.

Emotional Freedom Technique, a psychotherapeutic alternative medicine tool, also considered to be pseudoscience by the mainstream medicine, is allegedly useful.

71

These treatment options are not mutually exclusive. Often a therapist will suggest multiple treatments.

Epidemiology

Phobias are a common form of anxiety disorders. An American study by the National Institute of Mental Health (NIMH) found that between 8.7% and 18.1% of Americans suffer from phobias. Broken down by age and gender, the study found that phobias were the most common mental illness among women in all age groups and the second most common illness among men older than 25.

Non-psychological conditions

The word "phobia" may also signify conditions other than fear. For example, although the term *hydrophobia* means a fear of water, it may also mean inability to drink water due to an illness, or may be used to describe a chemical compound which repels water. It was also once used as a synonym for rabies, as an aversion to water is one of its symptoms. Likewise, the term photophobia may be used to define a physical complaint (i.e. aversion to light due to inflamed eyes or excessively dilated pupils) and does not necessarily indicate a fear of light.

Non-clinical uses of the term

It is possible for an individual to develop a phobia over virtually anything. The name of a phobia generally contains a Greek word for what the patient fears plus the suffix -*phobia*. Creating these terms is something of a word game. Few of these terms are found in medical literature. However, this does not necessarily make it a non-psychological condition.

Terms for prejudice or discrimination

A number of terms with the suffix -phobia are used non-clinically but have gained public acceptance, though they are often considered buzzwords. Such terms are primarily understood as negative attitudes towards certain categories of people or other things, used in an analogy with the medical usage of the term. Usually these kinds of "phobias" are described as fear, dislike, disapproval, prejudice, hatred, discrimination, or hostility towards the object of the "phobia". Often this attitude is based on prejudices and is a particular case of most xenophobia. These non-clinical phobias are typically used as labels cast on someone by another person or some other group.

Below are some examples:

- Chemophobia – prejudice against artificial substances in favour of "natural" substances.
- Ephebiphobia – fear or dislike of youth or adolescents.
- Homophobia – fear or dislike of homosexuals or homosexuality.
- Xenophobia – fear or dislike of strangers or the unknown, sometimes used to describe nationalistic political beliefs and movements. It is also used in fictional work to describe the fear or dislike of space aliens.

Everyone, from the youngest child to the oldest adult, experiences anxieties and fears at one time or another. Feeling anxious in a particularly uncomfortable situation never feels very good. However, with kids, such feelings are not only normal, they're also necessary. Dealing with anxieties can prepare young people to handle the unsettling experiences and challenging situations of life.

Many Anxieties and Fears Are Normal

Anxiety is defined as "apprehension without apparent cause." It usually occurs when there's no immediate threat to a person's safety or well being, but the threat feels real.

Anxiety makes someone want to escape the situation — fast. The heart beats quickly, the body might begin to perspire, and "butterflies" in the stomach soon follow. However, a little bit of anxiety can actually help people stay alert and focused.

Having fears or anxieties about certain things can also be helpful because it makes kids behave in a safe way. For example, a kid with a fear of fire would avoid playing with matches.

The nature of anxieties and fears change as kids grow and develop:

Babies experience stranger anxiety, clinging to parents when confronted by people they don't recognize.

Toddlers around 10 to 18 months old experience separation anxiety, becoming emotionally distressed when one or both parents leave.

Kids ages 4 through 6 have anxiety about things that aren't based in reality, such as fears of monsters and ghosts.

Kids ages 7 through 12 often have fears that reflect real circumstances that may happen to them, such as bodily injury and natural disaster.

As kids grow, one fear may disappear or replace another. For example, a child who couldn't sleep with the light off at age 5 may enjoy a ghost story at a slumber party years later. And some fears may extend only to one particular kind of stimulus. In other words, a child may want to pet a lion at the zoo but wouldn't dream of going near the neighbor's dog.

Signs of Anxiety

Typical childhood fears change with age. They include fear of strangers, heights, darkness, animals, blood, insects, and being left alone. Kids often learn to fear a specific object or situation after having an unpleasant experience, such as a dog bite or an accident.

Separation anxiety is common when young children are starting school, whereas adolescents may experience anxiety related to social acceptance and academic achievement.

If anxious feelings persist, they can take a toll on a child's sense of well being. The anxiety associated with social avoidance can have long-term effects. For example, a child with fear of being rejected can fail to learn important social skills, causing social isolation.

Many adults are tormented by fears that stem from childhood experiences. An adult's fear of public speaking may be the result of embarrassment in front of peers many years before. It's important for parents to recognize and identify the signs and symptoms of kids' anxieties so that fears don't get in the way of everyday life.

Some signs that a child may be anxious about something may include:

becoming clingy, impulsive, or distracted
nervous movements, such as temporary twitches
problems getting to sleep and/or staying asleep longer than usual
sweaty hands
accelerated heart rate and breathing
nausea
headaches
stomachaches

Apart from these signs, parents can usually tell when their child is feeling excessively uneasy about something. Lending a sympathetic ear is always helpful, and sometimes just talking about the fear can help a child move beyond it.

Focusing on Anxieties, Fears, or Phobias

Try to answer the following questions honestly:

Is your child's fear and behavior related to it typical for your child's age? If the answer to this question is yes, it's a good bet that your child's fears will resolve before they become a serious cause for concern. This isn't to say that the anxiety should be discounted or ignored; rather, it should be considered as a factor in your child's normal development.

Many kids experience age-appropriate fears, such as being afraid of the dark. Most, with some reassurance and perhaps a night-light, will overcome or outgrow it. However, if they continue to have trouble or there's anxiety about other things, the intervention may have to be more intensive.

What are the symptoms of the fear, and how do they affect your child's personal, social, and academic functioning? If symptoms can be identified and considered in light of your child's everyday activities, adjustments can be made to alleviate some of the stress factors.

Does the fear seem unreasonable in relation to the reality of the situation; and could it be a sign of a more serious problem? If your child's fear seems out of proportion to the cause of the stress, this may signal the need to seek outside help, such as a counselor, psychiatrist, or psychologist.

Parents should look for patterns. If an isolated incident is resolved, don't make it more significant than it is. But if a pattern emerges that's persistent or pervasive, you should take action. If you don't, the phobia is likely to continue to affect your child.

Contact your doctor and/or a mental health professional who has expertise in working with kids and adolescents.

Helping Your Child

Parents can help kids develop the skills and confidence to overcome fears so that they don't evolve into phobic reactions.

To help your child deal with fears and anxieties:

Recognize that the fear is real. As trivial as a fear may seem, it feels real to your child and it's causing him or her to feel anxious and afraid. Being able to talk about fears helps — words often take some of the power out of the negative feeling. If you talk about it, it can become less powerful.

Never belittle the fear as a way of forcing your child to overcome it. Saying, "Don't be ridiculous! There are no monsters in your closet!" may get your child to go to bed, but it won't make the fear go away.

Don't cater to fears, though. If your child doesn't like dogs, don't cross the street deliberately to avoid one. This will just reinforce that dogs should be feared and avoided. Provide support and gentle care as you approach the feared object or situation with your child.

Teach kids how to rate fear. A child who can visualize the intensity of the fear on a scale of 1 to 10, with 10 being the strongest, may be able to "see" the fear as less intense than first imagined. Younger kids can think about how "full of fear" they are, with being full "up to my knees" as not so scared, "up to my stomach" as more frightened, and "up to my head" as truly petrified.

Teach coping strategies. Try these easy-to-implement techniques. Using you as "home base," the child can venture out toward the feared object, and then return to you for safety before venturing out again. The child can also learn some positive self-statements, such as "I can do this" and "I will be OK" to say to himself or herself when feeling anxious. Relaxation techniques are helpful, including visualization (of floating on a cloud or lying on a beach, for example) and deep breathing (imagining that the lungs are balloons and letting them slowly deflate).

What is child anxiety?

All humans experience anxiety, it serves as a means of protection and can often enhance our performance in stressful situations. Children who are able to experience the slight rush of anxiety that often occurs prior to a math test or a big track race often can enhance their performance. However, experiencing too much anxiety or general nervousness, at inappropriate times, can be extremely distressing and interfering. Although children have fears of specific objects, the feeling of anxiety is more general... children may feel constantly "keyed up" or extremely alert. Given the wide range of tasks children must accomplish throughout their childhood, it is important to be sure that their level of anxiety does not begin to interfere with their ability to function. If it does, it is important that they begin to learn some skills for coping more efficiently with their anxious feelings.

What are fears and phobias?

Children's fears are often natural, and arise at specific times in their development. Children may develop fears from a traumatic experience (e.g. traumatic dog attack), but for some children, there is no clear event that causes the fear to arise. Some children become fearful simply by watching another child acting scared. Some children may refuse to sleep alone due to fears of creatures in their closet, while other children report feeling afraid of the dark. Children's fears are often associated with avoidance, discomfort, and physical complaints, such as rapid heart beat, stomach

77

distress, sweaty palms, or trembling. Researchers have found certain fears arise at specific ages in all children, and these fears tend to disappear naturally with time, as the child grows older. When children's fears persist beyond the age when they are appropriate, and begin to interfere with their daily functioning, they are called phobias. Typically, children who are experiencing a phobia should be referred for treatment by a psychologist.

Which of my child's fears are normal?

Most children, when asked, are able to report having several fears at any given age. Some research shows that 90% of children between the ages of 2-14 have at least one specific fear. If your child's fear is not interfering with his/her daily life (e.g., sleep, school performance, social activities) , or your family's life, then most likely you will not need to bring your child to a psychologist for help. Here are a list of fears that are found to be VERY COMMON for children at specific ages:

INFANTS/TODDLERS (ages 0-2 years) loud noises, strangers, separation from parents, large objects

PRESCHOOLERS (3-6 years) imaginary figures (e.g., ghosts, monsters, supernatural beings, the dark, noises, sleeping alone, thunder, floods)

SCHOOL AGED CHILDREN/ADOLESCENTS (7-16 years) more realistic fears (e.g., physical injury, health, school performance, death, thunderstorms, earthquakes, floods.

WHAT DO CHILDREN FEAR?

The objects and situations that children fear vary a good deal. When very young children show fear it can be hard to judge exactly what is causing it, and many parents underestimate the number of things that frighten their children. In one study of 'just-fours', parents reported that two-thirds of children had recurrent fears, and other research points to a typical pattern and there are some fears such as as snakes, spiders and heights that seem common to us as a species. Parents should always be aware that some intense fears are quite a natural developmental stage and will ease naturally. The following is a general list of normal fears:

Age 2-4: fear of animals, loud noises, being left alone, inconsistent discipline, toilet training, bath, bedtime, monsters and ghosts, bed wetting, disabled people, death and injury.

Age 4-6: fear of darkness and imaginary creatures. Also animals, bedtime, monsters and ghosts. Other fears, such as of strangers seem to be persistent. 'Stranger fear' would probably be called 'shyness', while fear of snakes tends not to decrease much, if at all, during this period. Children at this age may also fear loss of a parent, death, injury and divorce.

Beyond these ages, irrational fears tend to decline rapidly, though there may be further peaks to do with other situations, e.g. age 9-11: fear of school; fear of blood and injury.

Older children tend to worry more about death and related topics such as nuclear war. Up to age 11 boys and girls tend to be equally represented in the 'fear tables'; after 11 years boys lose their fears more rapidly than girls.

It has been suggested by some research that children between the ages of three and six; sometimes confuse reality, dreams and fantasy. This concept has been challenged in recent years, so it is not safe to believe that everything that the child of this age fears is just something they will grow out of. Young children may also sometimes believe that inanimate or non-living objects have lifelike qualities. They may too have inaccurate concepts of size relationships (monsters that can come up through plug-hole for example). They may also lack an accurate understanding of cause and effect and often perceive themselves as helpless and powerless, without effective means to control what is happening to them.8 year-olds will probably have fragments of earlier fears but additional ones will tend to be more rationally based and will possibly include fear being late for school, social rejection, criticism, new situations, adoption, burglars, personal danger and war. 9 and 10 year-olds are also likely to fear divorce, personal danger and war and these three are very likely to continue as fear problems into the mid teens. This age group might also fear blood and injury.

11 and 12 year-olds might fear animals, kidnapping, being alone in the dark and injections. Marks states that beyond this age boys lose their fears more readily than girls. 13 year-olds seem to fear heights as well as the three mentioned above.

14-16 year-olds will tend to have a wide range of rational or almost rational fears which might include: injury, kidnapping, being alone in the dark, injections, heights, terrorism, plane or car crashes, sexual relations, drug use, public speaking, school performance, crowds, gossip and divorce.

These childhood fears are not that different from those of adults. The most common adult fears are: public speaking, making mistakes, failure, disapproval, rejection, angry people, being alone, darkness, dentists, injections, hospitals, taking tests, open wounds and blood, police, dogs, spiders and deformed people.

As will be noted from the above, many childhood problems wax and wane as a normal part of development and a sensitivity in a certain area might be aggravated by a current problem so that this particular child temporarily 'falls back' into an earlier level of fear when faced with a trauma or severe family or school problems.

WHAT ARE THE SYMPTOMS OF PHOBIA?

In adults, phobias produce all the unpleasant physical symptoms of 'normal' fear:

* heart palpitations
* feeling sick
* chest pains
* difficulty breathing
* dizziness
* 'jelly legs'
* feeling 'unreal'
* intense sweating
* feeling faint
* dry throat

* restricted or 'fuzzy' vision or hearing.

In severe cases, people may feel certain that they are about to die, go mad, or lose control of themselves and injure someone, or do something disgusting and humiliating. Most of all they feel an overpowering urge to 'escape' from the situation they are in. Children are more likely to cry, shout or scream, or simply run away when confronted by the things they fear, though they may also be sick or go rigid. Paleness, perspiration and trembling are also signs of severe anxiety.

The level of symptoms that children with phobias experience varies a great deal, from very mild anxiety to very severe panic and terror. A mild degree of nervousness in particular situations is not usually a problem, but it is only a matter of degree, and at the other end of the scale there are children who have full-scale panic attacks when in the dreaded situation, and soon refuse to enter it altogether because of the terror that grips them at such times.

Phobias aren't just severe anxiety: the anxiety is turned into a phobia by avoidance. In the early stages of a phobia the child's parents sometimes try to tackle his or her fears head on by forcing him or her to enter the feared situation. If this works, the phobia can be overcome. If it doesn't, this is only likely to strengthen the fears and make the child want to avoid the phobic situation even more. It also risks destroying the child's confidence in its parents.

Avoidance is attractive because it brings a reduction of the tension; thus it rapidly becomes a habit. As with adults, avoiding the situations that make them feel frightened makes children more sensitive to those situations, and 'conditions' them to fear them even more.

This is why phobias can be such a big problem. Because we tend to avoid the things we fear, the fear can worsen very rapidly. To recover, we need to put that process into reverse, but the fear reaction is virtually automatic, and very difficult to control. It is a reaction inherited from our early history as a species, when we needed some instinctive protection to balance out our curiosity and tendency to flirt with danger. Fortunately, humans learn quickly and can train themselves to respond positively to threats, and not to react with terror to things which prove, with experience, to be harmless.

IT CAN'T JUST BE ANXIETY, CAN IT?

A child with severe phobic symptoms has an anxiety condition. This is much worse than just being nervous or 'a bit of a worrier'. Anxiety at this level can be as disabling as many physical diseases. However, because it seems unreasonable for someone to react so strongly to such ordinary situations, many parents may suspect a more 'logical' explanation - perhaps a serious physical or mental illness. Then the child may become a frequent visitor to the doctor's surgery and undergo a long series of medical tests, all of which draw a blank.

It often comes as a great relief to parents when they learn that the problem is not a brain tumour, psychosis etc., and that the nasty and frightening symptoms are in fact caused by anxiety. However, there is always the remote possibility that the child also has a medical condition, and this is one reason why we always recommend parents of phobic children to keep in touch with their GP.

HOW CAN CHILDREN'S FEARS BE TREATED?

The first thing to be considered is whether or not the phobia impacts strongly on the child's life. If it does not interfere with day-to-day functioning then it might be worth considering allowing nature to take its course. If there is a level of handicap or severe distress, then treatment is indicated.

Persistent fears in children can be treated in much the same way as they are in adults; that is by desensitisation through being exposed to the feared situation. However, as children's fears are often volatile and transitory the child's previous record with fears should be considered before launching into an elaborate treatment programme. As already said, most fears will cease to be a problem without any need for treatment, and there is always the risk of teaching the child a new way of getting attention if every expression of fear brings a dramatic response from a parent. (Of course, if a child feels the need to use 'fears' as a way to be noticed, this might indicate different kinds of problem within the family.)

Nobody with a phobia responds to punishment or obtains the slightest improvement from being 'talked out of it'. Children in particular seem to respond best to being helped to increase their skill and competence, and being encouraged to take part in activities that will involve the thing they fear. With young children especially, practical activities that involve exposure could also be turned into a game, since most children respond better to play than to work. With a fear of bees, for instance:

first the bee is shown in a sealed bottle, some distance away

then it is brought closer; then closer (the child can be rewarded with a small treat for every shoe's length closer he or she is prepared to approach the bottle - or allows the bottle to approach, if that is less stressful). Eventually the child can be helped to touch the bottle, with a grand prize for this. Other exposure 'steps' could include walking in the garden (accompanied at first) when bees are about, with an escape route clearly established to build confidence. if the parent is feeling brave, further exposure could be undertaken by 'modelling', i.e. doing the feared thing and showing the child in practice that there is no need to be afraid. In the case of a bee this might involve letting the bee alight on their clothing, with the child safely distant.In extreme cases of phobia in children a therapist might use relaxation, videos and 'fantasy exposure' (helping the child to face the dreaded situation in his or her imagination) before attempting live exposure work.

Talking help

Most children do not want to upset their parents and may be resistant to talking about the intensity of their feelings. If this is the case, one technique suggested by Anxiety Care is to ask the child what he or she thinks a close friend would be feeling in this situation. This doesn't work, of course, if the friend is perceived to be tough, but if the child can be helped to explore this cared-for person's possible responses in similar situations, where he or she was afraid, this can establish the level of fear that the phobic child accepts as 'normal'. Parents can sometimes be horrified at the fear levels uncovered in this way and it is important that an over reaction that involves shame and feelings of worthlessness as a parent do not become involved. If it does, this will only cloud the issue and unbalance the necessary socialising and discipline that the child needs in the rest of his or her daily life.

When the child resists support, it can become very difficult. Where very negative thinking is involved, the parent can try to help by gently challenging the child's thought processes. This is described in 'Poor Thinking' on this site. Obviously a heavy challenge is rarely likely to work with a very young child and the parent needs to work out the best way to approach the problem: in some way helping the child to look at his or her thoughts and beliefs in a way that is challenging, not threatening. If the child refuses all help then the parent could usefully talk to a doctor or therapist without the child being present in order to learn ways to apply help at such time that the child is willing to accept it.

Depression

Sometimes depression occurs alongside a severe phobia. The problem here is that depression undermines: it takes away the will to try to overcome the phobia and may even make the sufferer feel that he or she is helpless against it. Where depression is suspected the GP must become involved. If the depression is mild or moderate, the child will probably receive help focused on the anxiety with concurrent support for the depression. If the depression is judged to be severe, the focus will be on treating the depression.

Medication

Drugs are rarely the first treatment of choice for young children. In the developing brain the neurotransmitting system seems to be particularly sensitive to medication so it is unlikely that a doctor would suggest medication early on in treatment for a very young child. If it is considered, the dosages would have to be very carefully monitored.

SCHOOL PHOBIA (SCHOOL REFUSING)

The number of children who dislike school and avoid it whenever possible is probably more than 5% of the school-age population, but less than 1% could genuinely be called 'school phobic'. School phobia, also called 'school refusal' is commoner among boys, and the peak onset in Britain is at the age of 11-12 years. This is perhaps not surprising, since this is the age when most children move from primary to secondary school, and therefore experience great changes in their lives.

There are also smaller peaks at the age of 5-7 years old, where separation from the mother may be a primary cause (See the article on separation anxiety on this site); and at 14, where it is more likely to be associated with a psychiatric disorder such as depression.

Some older adolescents and young adults may experience fears of college or work that resemble school phobia; most of these will have been school refusers when children.

Sometimes school refusing begins suddenly, for instance after a prolonged absence from school due to illness; following an abrupt change of school or class; after school holidays - or even after a weekend. However, the actual event immediately before school refusal is unlikely to be the sole cause of the problem, though it might have been the last straw on top of a lot of other things. These additional situations could include family problems; difficulties at school; anxiety about puberty; other sexual matters; general difficulty with social situations; anxiety about being separated from the parents (mainly the mother); bereavement; or depression.

However, most cases of school refusal seem to develop slowly. Reluctance to attend gradually increases, with visible signs of anxiety that grow more obvious as the child is pressured to go. Sometimes the child will deny that he or she is afraid, but signs such as paleness, trembling and frequent urination may be very obvious to the parent. Typically the child will complain of bodily pains, stomach trouble or nausea in the early morning. These problems usually cease abruptly if the child is allowed to stay at home, and re-appear when he or she is once again pressured to go to school.

Some children will simply refuse to go to school, offering no reason. Others might complain of bullying, or of being unable to get on with teachers or do the school work. Some may express fears about undressing in front of other children, or of making a spectacle of themselves by fainting, vomiting or losing control of their bowels. Less often they may mention fears of something happening to one or both of their parents while they are at school, or simply of feeling `unsafe' when far from home.

Children deal with their fear of attending school in many ways. Some may go through the morning ritual almost normally, but are then unable to leave the house, or turn back before reaching school. Others may flatly refuse to get out of bed, or lock themselves in somewhere, or run off until they feel it is safe to return home. Some will gladly put up with punishment as the price of not going, and many will promise (and mean it at the time) to go 'this afternoon' or 'tomorrow' if they are only allowed to stay at home now. Some children have been known to threaten, or even attempt, suicide when they felt totally trapped by the situation.

PHOBIA OR TRUANCY?

School phobia is sometimes confused with truancy - even by teachers and educational workers. However, truants do not usually express or display such high levels of anxiety, and nor do they flatly refuse to attend school. It is just that there are other things they would rather be doing. They are more likely to pretend to set off for school, and then disappear on the way, or during the day, returning home at the normal time, so that parents are often the last to find out what is happening. Truants also tend to become involved in other delinquent behaviour. They may also come from disadvantaged areas and homes where there is not enough discipline, caring, or simple parental interest. Their school work is likely to be rather poor and they will probably show little interest in what the school thinks of them.

This is in sharp contrast to the typical school refuser, who comes from a stable home with both parents present and caring (if sometimes over-protective) and who is often described as "always such a good boy/girl - never any trouble before this". Typical refusers may also be sensitive to the point of timidity, being unduly wounded by adverse comments from teachers, and have unrealistically high goals for themselves; they may then become excessively upset at their perceived failures.

TREATMENT FOR SCHOOL REFUSAL

Anxiety Care receives many letters and phone calls from parents of school refusers. Besides the anxiety and confusion, many share a feeling of guilt. They have been told, or have read, that it is "all their fault" for making a "mummy's boy (or girl)" out of the child. In our culture, that usually means 'wimpish' and 'inadequate'. Parental reactions can then be deep shame or anger and a closing of family ranks. None of this is conducive to helping the child out of the problem.

Although 'separation anxiety' (difficulty in leaving mother) can be a major factor in school refusal for 5 to 7 year-olds, it is not necessarily significant for older children.

'Real' fears of such things as being bullied, PE and games, unfriendly teachers, the size of the school, and other personal and family difficulties, might be the dominant factors. Several cases brought to Anxiety Care have been triggered (or 'last-strawed') by a death in the family. Sometimes it was not a close relative, or even a human being that died; but for an 11 or 12 year-old this may have been the first time that the finality of death came home to them; and this can be a shock. Even if the experience wasn't particularly traumatic, it is never safe to assume that children will deal with such a loss as an adult would.

Children may also react to loss of friends through moving to a new school or area in the same way that they would to a bereavement. A good therapist would not jump to conclusions about reasons, but would make a systematic investigation of all the possible factors - child, family and school.

PROFESSIONAL THERAPY FOR SCHOOL REFUSING

Parents cannot afford to allow school refusal to be ignored or treated in a haphazard and ineffectual manner. The law requires a child to be educated, and most parents are not able to pick and choose where this takes place. If children do not go to school, parents may be taken to court, and there is even the (very slight) risk of the child being taken into care. Nobody wants this to happen, so professional help is usually readily available, and it is vital for parents to make the best use of it.

Most current treatments for school refusing are carried out around the home and the school by clinical child psychologists. They will involve helping the child to deal with anxiety symptoms in the situation where they developed, while getting the child back to school as quickly as possible. Inpatient treatment compares poorly with this kind of 'live' support, though a small minority of children do fare better away from home. Some parents may be tempted to take their child out of the school system altogether, but research shows that temporary home tuition is not a useful road to recovery, and works against the child's early return to school. Permanent withdrawal, even if some children do better academically, and feel more content outside the school system, has some dangers. The child with low social skills may not learn how to relate to the peer group, which can become a major problem. The child may also never resolve the underlying problems that generated, or were part of, the school phobia.

They may thus become prime candidates for a similar anxiety disorder later in life when faced with going to college, or to work. They may also be so handicapped by lack of the social and 'peer' learning gained at school that character traits such as timidity, over-sensitivity, and the tendency to have unrealistic expectations of themselves and others, may become a permanent barrier between the young adult and the rest of the world. The problem with setting a goal of 'the child returning to school as quickly as possible' is deciding how soon to aim for. The therapist's personal beliefs and the extent of the child's anxiety will be the main factors here. However, whether the period is short or long, all therapists will have a series of priorities. They will: work at establishing a good, trusting relationship with the child and the family clarify the situations that actually create anxiety desensitize the child to these situations by getting the child to imagine the dreaded events, with relaxation techniques, and simply by talking about it lastly, they will help the child to confront the situations 'live'.

THERAPISTS AND PARENTS

Therapists are well aware that they need the full support of the child's family, and that there can be much confusion, anger, guilt and plain misconception to work through before therapy proper can begin. They would spend time with the parents, trying to assess how much bearing their behaviour and reactions have on the school refusal problem.

They would probably meet with the parents alone, so that other problems which could be affecting the child might be resolved without the child being drawn into them (or feeling to blame for them). They would also talk through worries such as parents feeling cruel and guilty about forcing the child to go to school. Where parents are uneasy about seeming to criticise teachers, or staff feel threatened or irritated by the idea that their school is a 'dreaded place', they would also act as go-between.

The therapist would also help the parents find the best ways to deal with: the child's tantrums, complaints about illness, refusal to talk about the problem (or insistence on doing so) redressing the balance if the child had begun to dominate the family through the phobia ways to avoid escalating threats and/or polarising into 'protecting mother' and 'threatening father' that can be so damaging in the families of school refusers.

Towards the end of the treatment, with the child ready to attend school, the therapist would also discuss the best times to return, such as after a weekend or a holiday, rather than in midweek, which might arouse more comment from other children. And they would work out, perhaps using role play, the responses the child might use to those making fun of his or her absence. After the child has returned to school, they would go on to help the parents recognise danger points in the future, and encourage them to use the 'management' techniques they have learned. Live exposure to the dreaded situation is part of overcoming all phobias. However, simply dragging a child to school would not be appropriate in most cases. While school may be the focus of fear, most school refusers get to that point via a number of 'stressor' situations working together. So before the journey to school is attempted, the various fears already mentioned have to be faced. Nevertheless, the journey to school has to be undertaken sooner or later, and this can be a very dramatic time, when the parents' anxiety is almost as high as the child's. Parent and therapist have to be clear how to deal with this. A good therapist will have explained that all 'exposure work' is built round the child's actual anxiety level, not what it should be or could be. This will ease parents' fears of the child experiencing a total collapse or breakdown. A strategy would be worked out in advance for certain situations, for example: with a young child, the parents would not linger within sight of the classroom, fuelling the child's anxiety as well as their own if the child was to be physically restrained from escaping, the parents wouldn't let the child think that a little more hysteria might bring them leaping to the defence there would be a planned response if the child should run home. It is extraordinarily hard for parents to stand by while their children suffer, even when they know it is necessary and temporary. Therapists work closely with parents, and they understand how important it is for the family to be able to support the child as he or she gradually comes to terms with school life.

Most children experience some nervousness at the beginning of a new school year. New teachers, new classes and a whole new routine can leave even the most even-tempered child frazzled and exhausted in the first few weeks. Most of the time, children settle into a routine and quickly work through their early jitters.

For some children, however, normal anxiety gives way to more serious fears. Phobias are common in children. In fact, the majority of specific phobias appear by the time the sufferer is seven years old. Fortunately, most childhood phobias respond well to treatment. Children may not share their fears, so it often falls to parents to monitor their kids. Here are some things to look for in children of various ages.

Elementary School

According to developmental psychologist Jean Piaget, children are in the "concrete operational stage" of cognitive development from the ages of approximately seven to eleven. Their fears tend to reflect the concrete way in which they see their environment. Common phobias in elementary school aged children include fears of thunderstorms, animals, and the dark. School-related phobias may also develop, such as a fear of bigger kids or a fear of a teacher that is perceived as "mean."

Children of this age often demonstrate their anxiety by regressing. They may become clingy, refuse to go into the classroom without a parent and cry or throw tantrums. They may also freeze or run when confronted with the feared situation. Physical complaints such as stomach aches are also common, and usually follow a pattern.

Middle School

Again, according to Piaget, most children enter the "formal operational stage" of development near the beginning of their middle school years. Pre-teens begin to understand abstract topics such as love, and begin to explore "shades of gray." It's also a time of immense pressure for many kids, as they struggle to establish their identities, forge more adult friendships and begin to plan for their futures.

The most common phobias in this age group tend to focus on school-related topics. "School phobia" is a general term that may apply to any fears that make the child reluctant to go to school. School phobia is thought to be related to separation anxiety, but may also stem from bullying or humiliation, or a simple reaction to new pressures.

Many kids of this age react to their fears through defiance. They may become argumentative or withdrawn, develop friendships with troublemakers, skip school or even turn to alcohol or drugs. Some children regress instead, becoming clingy and overly dependent on the parent.

High School

High school is a whirlwind time of changes and pressures. Kids of this age are torn between wanting to become adults and wanting to extend their childhoods. They worry about their grades, wonder if they will get into good colleges and struggle to develop adult relationships with their friends and dating partners.

Agoraphobia and social phobia are most common among this age group. Social phobia can be related to the body image issues that plague many teens. It may be restricted to a single situation, such as a fear of speaking in front of the class, or may be all-encompassing, making teens scared to be seen in public. Agoraphobia may develop out of an untreated social phobia or another disorder, or may appear alone. Agoraphobic teens may severely restrict their activities out of a fear of losing control in public.

Teens generally display many of the same phobia symptoms as adults. They may refuse to participate in certain activities. They may shake, sweat or show signs of illness before or during a confrontation with the feared activity. Teens may also turn to alcohol or drugs as an escape. They may spend a great deal of time alone, and may gradually develop depression or other disorders.

Helping Your Child Confront a Phobia

Although some phobias spontaneously go away without treatment, others will gradually worsen until treatment is obtained. However, it can be difficult for parents to know how to help, especially if the child is reluctant to discuss the situation.

If you notice a change in your child's behavior, talk to him or her about your concerns. Keep your tone light and friendly, as kids are extremely perceptive to the moods of others. Ask him directly about his fears, but avoid making accusations.

Be supportive - within reason. Many parents' first reaction is to force the child to confront the fear. While flooding can be an effective professional technique, it should not be tried by anyone who is not trained in its use. Forcing your child into a feared situation could cause psychological damage.

Yet, on the other hand, don't be *too* supportive. Some parents go to the opposite extreme, shielding their children from any possibility of confronting the feared situation. This can reinforce the phobia, making it much more difficult to treat.

Whether to seek treatment can be a difficult call for parents. If your child has a specific phobia that is not greatly impacting his or her life, you might want to wait it out. Specific phobias in children are generally not diagnosed until they have been present for at least six months. In the meantime, be calm and reassuring with your child, and help him or her talk through the fear.

Social phobia and agoraphobia should be treated more aggressively, as should persistent specific phobias. The family doctor is a great place to start. He or she can ensure that there is nothing medically wrong with the child, and provide a reference to a trusted therapist.

Treatment may take many forms, depending on your child's needs. Play therapy for younger children and medication are especially common. Look for a therapist that makes both you and your child comfortable. You will be an important part of your child's phobia treatment.

When a child doesn't want to go to school, it is often assumed by school professionals the reason lies at home. Perhaps the child is afraid to leave home out of an unrealistic belief he or she must stay behind to mind the store, or to guard against some danger. The hypothesis is the child feels unbearably anxious unless he or she stays home, where the parents' well-being may be confirmed. The child's parents, on the other hand, may search for something in school that has intimidated their child. A school psychologist understands that school avoidance is probably the result of many factors, and the child may be reacting to both home and school stressors.

Current thinking about school phobia suggests there are some children who refuse to attend school because of separation anxiety. These are mostly younger children who are less accustomed to being away from home.

The majority of children who refuse school, however, are between eight and thirteen years old. Some are trying to avoid uncomfortable feelings associated with school. They tend to be sensitive, overactive boys and girls who don't know how to deal with their emotions. They may fear being criticized or evaluated. A few are truly frightened by a particular activity, such as riding the school bus or attending an assembly.

Many of these children do attend school but with great discomfort. They tend to be highly anxious and lack the skills needed to handle social interactions. Perhaps they have had negative experiences in the past and are afraid something else will happen.

Research indicates many children experience school events as stressful enough to produce such symptoms as withdrawal, aggression, moodiness or anxiety. Studies conducted at the National Center for the Study of Corporal Punishment (reported in the *Monitor*, the newspaper of the American Psychological Association) indicates many of these events involve disciplinary methods which are punitive in nature and attack the child's self esteem. A child's behavior may even resemble symptoms of post-traumatic stress disorder. In this condition, memories of a traumatic event continue to interfere with daily functioning, long after the actual event took place.

While severe stress responses may be unusual, any child who does not want to go to school is experiencing stress, and an important part of solving the problem is for the adults involved to assess what may have gone wrong. When a child seeks to avoid school, the parents are advised to quickly request consultation with both the classroom teacher and the school psychologist. If this is done, parents, teacher and psychologist may explore clues from both home and school to determine how the child's needs are not being met. While most children are adaptive and resourceful and able to adjust to a certain amount of challenge, there are limits to adaptation. Children whose skills are weak in areas needed for school success may encounter demands beyond their abilities. Sensitive children who are highly in tune with others may encounter an experience which overloads their finely-tuned empathies. Whatever the cause, the parents need to see themselves as part of a professional team working to solve the problem.

But first of all, parents must bring the child to school. They will probably be strongly ambivalent about subjecting the child to what seems like a piece of unbearable stress. However, by working with the school psychologist to find ways to modify school and home environments for the child's benefit, some of the discomfort will be resolved. Sometimes simple interventions, such as a planned focus on the child's positive behaviors, or special time with an important person in the child's life, may help the child comfortably resume going to school. At school, short-term counseling, opportunities to engage in favorite activities, or a chance to earn a privilege could be options. If necessary, the psychologist will also help find a therapist to work with both the child and the family.

The experience of joining with school personnel to successfully reintegrate a phobic child into the school will allow parents to learn what works and what doesn't for their boy or girl. They will have an ally in the school psychologist, who will act as a liaison among the various people involved. If the child has other difficulties beyond school refusal, they will be addressed. Intervention will give the child a chance to benefit from the educational environment and to master academic tasks in a supportive and encouraging setting where the child may thrive.

Avoidant personality disorder

Avoidant personality disorder (or anxious personality disorder) is a personality disorder recognized in the Diagnostic and Statistical Manual of Mental Disorders handbook in a person characterized by a pervasive pattern of social inhibition, feelings of inadequacy, extreme sensitivity to negative evaluation, and avoidance of social interaction.

People with Avoidant personality disorder often consider themselves to be socially inept or personally unappealing, and avoid social interaction for fear of being ridiculed, humiliated, rejected, or disliked.

Avoidant personality disorder is usually first noticed in early adulthood. Childhood emotional neglect and peer group rejection are both associated with an increased risk for the development of AvPD.

There is controversy as to whether Avoidant personality disorder is a distinct disorder from generalized social phobia and it is contended by some that they are merely different conceptualisations of the same disorder, where Avoidant personality disorder may represent the more severe form. This is argued as generalized social phobia and Avoidant personality disorder have a similar diagnostic criteria and may share a similar causation, subjective experience, course, treatment, and identical underlying personality features, such as shyness.

Signs and symptoms

People with Avoidant personality disorder are preoccupied with their own shortcomings and form relationships with others only if they believe they will not be rejected. Loss and rejection are so painful that these individuals will choose to be lonely rather than risk trying to connect with others.

- Hypersensitivity to rejection/criticism
- Self-imposed social isolation
- Extreme shyness or anxiety in social situations, though the person feels a strong desire for close relationships
- Avoids physical contact because it has been associated with an unpleasant or painful stimulus
- Avoids interpersonal relationships
- Feelings of inadequacy
- Severe low self-esteem
- Self-loathing
- Mistrust of others

- Emotional distancing related to intimacy
- Highly self-conscious
- Self-critical about their problems relating to others
- Problems in occupational functioning
- Lonely self-perception, although others may find the relationship with them meaningful
- Feeling inferior to others
- In some more extreme cases — agoraphobia
- Utilizes fantasy as a form of escapism and to interrupt painful thoughts

Causes

Apart from the above, other causes of Avoidant personality disorder are not clearly defined, and may be influenced by a combination of social, genetic, and psychological factors. The disorder may be related to temperamental factors that are inherited. Specifically, various anxiety disorders in childhood and adolescence have been associated with a temperament characterized by behavioral inhibition, including features of being shy, fearful, and withdrawn in new situations. These inherited characteristics may give an individual a genetic predisposition towards AvPD. Childhood emotional neglect and peer group rejection are both associated with an increased risk for the development of AvPD.

Psychologist Theodore Millon identified four subtypes of avoidant personality disorder. Any individual avoidant may exhibit none or one of the following:

- conflicted avoidant - including negativistic features

The conflicted avoidant feels ambivalent towards themselves and others. They can idealize those close to them but under stress they may feel under-appreciated or misunderstood and wish to hurt others in revenge. They may be perceived as petulant or to be sulking

- hypersensitive avoidant - including paranoid features

The hypersensitive avoidant experiences paranoia, mistrustfulness and fear, but to a lesser extent than an individual with paranoid personality disorder.[20] They may be perceived as petulant or "high-strung".

- phobic avoidant - including dependent features

- self-deserting avoidant - including depressive features

Differential diagnosis

Research suggests that people with Avoidant personality disorder, in common with sufferers of chronic social anxiety disorder (also called social phobia), excessively monitor their own internal reactions when they are involved in social interaction. However, unlike social phobics, people with Avoidant personality disorder may also excessively monitor the reactions of the people with whom they are interacting.

The extreme tension created by this monitoring may account for the hesitant speech and taciturnity of many people with Avoidant personality disorder; they are so preoccupied with monitoring themselves and others that producing fluent speech is difficult.

Avoidant personality disorder is reported to be especially prevalent in people with anxiety disorders, although estimates of comorbidity vary widely due to differences in (among others) diagnostic instruments. Research suggests that approximately 10–50% of people who have panic disorder with agoraphobia have Avoidant personality disorder, as well as about 20–40% of people who have social phobia (social anxiety disorder).

Some studies report prevalence rates of up to 45% among people with generalized anxiety disorder and up to 56% of those with obsessive-compulsive disorder. Although it is not mentioned in the DSM-IV, earlier theorists have proposed a personality disorder which has a combination of features from borderline personality disorder and Avoidant personality disorder, called "avoidant-borderline mixed personality" (AvPD/BPD).

Treatment

Treatment of Avoidant personality disorder can employ various techniques, such as social skills training, cognitive therapy, exposure treatment to gradually increase social contacts, group therapy for practicing social skills, and sometimes drug therapy. A key issue in treatment is gaining and keeping the patient's trust, since people with Avoidant personality disorder will often start to avoid treatment sessions if they distrust the therapist or fear rejection. The primary purpose of both individual therapy and social skills group training is for individuals with Avoidant personality disorder to begin challenging their exaggerated negative beliefs about themselves.

Epidemiology

According to the DSM-IV-TR, Avoidant personality disorder occurs in approximately 0.5% to 1% of the general population. However, data from the 2001-02 National Epidemiologic Survery on Alcohol and Related Conditions indicates a prevalence rate of the disorder of 2.36% in the American general population. It is seen in about 10% of psychiatric outpatients.

History

The avoidant personality has been described in several sources as far back as the early 1900s, although it was not so named for some time. Swiss psychiatrist Eugen Bleuler described patients who exhibited signs of Avoidant personality disorder in his 1911 work *Dementia Praecox: Or the Group of Schizophrenias*. Avoidant and schizoid patterns were frequently confused or referred to synonymously until Kretschmer (1921), in providing the first relatively complete description, developed a distinction.

Treating Childhood Phobias - Phobia Treatments

Childhood Phobias Lead to Anxious Behavior in Adulthood

"Children who are not cured of their phobias run a great risk of developing other areas of anxiety later on," says Lena Reuterskiöld, of The Swedish Research Council.

"It's therefore important to find effective forms of treatment that can reduce this risk." She explains that certain one-session therapy treatment sessions are effective for various types of phobias.

The Research on Treatments for Phobias in Children

Reuterskiöld's research involved children and adolescents with various specific phobias in Stockholm, Sweden, and in Virginia in the United States. The treatment studied was a "one-session treatment" that was three hours long.

This phobia research showed that 55% of children who voluntarily signed up for this phobia treatment successfully overcame their anxiety attacks.

The "One-Session" Treatment for Kids With Phobias

This phobia treatment for children is accomplished in one session with a therapist. It isn't expensive (but the cost may flucuate with different psychologists or counselors). Unlike anxiety medication, this one-session therapy treatment for adolescents doesn't have side effects. Further, it's not associated with a specific culture, so doesn't need to be changed to fit a certain country or region.

In the session, a child slowly approaches whatever he/she is afraid of (alongside the therapist). This safe, controlled environment helps reduce anxiety attacks and feelings of fear. After the therapist interacts with the object of fear, the child is encouraged to do the same.

The theory behind this phobia for children is that they'll experience decreased anxiety, and learn that what they most fear will not occur (in psychology, this is exposure therapy or systematic desensitization). To reduce anxious behavior, it's important for children to spend an extended amount of time with the object they fear.

One-Session Therapy Treatment Works for Adults With Phobias

"One-session treatments have also proven to be effective over time," says Reuterskiöld. "Adults who have been treated with this method notice the effects of the treatment more than a year after the session. And nothing indicates that the effect would taper off sooner in children, which we assume will soon be confirmed by a follow-up study."

PERSONALITY DEVELOPMENT OF CHILDREN

Children are not just little adults. They go through typical characteristics of growth—intellectually, emotionally, and socially—on their way to becoming adults. When parents realize these things, there is less strain on both parents and children.

The following chart lists some common characteristics of children's behavior, arranged by broad age groupings, with reasons for that behavior and the implications that behavior may have on planning enjoyable and productive family home evenings. However, when considering any growth or behavior chart, remember that not every child will necessarily fit into described patterns. Individual children grow and develop differently and at different speeds. For instance, all children in one family will not walk or talk at the same age. Each child should be respected as an individual. The descriptions in this chart identify general behavior only, and you will note that the age groupings overlap.

Birth to 3 years of age

Characteristics

1. A child likes affection, being held and cuddled. He especially likes motion—being carried, tossed, and sitting on a lap.
2. He loses interest quickly and will interrupt conversations, stories, or activities with cries, noises, and wiggling. He enjoys simple, repeated gestures and touches, playing with objects, putting them in his mouth and throwing them.
3. A child stops "naughty" behavior when you tell him to, but he soon goes back to it as though he doesn't care what you want.

Reasons

1.Infants and young children learn trust and love first through touch. They are absorbed in exploring the world through their senses and movements, and they are gradually getting more control over their muscles.

2. Children at this age are only aware of their own viewpoint, wants, and experiences. Doing things over and over helps them learn about things.

3. Children have no understanding of rules and cannot understand how one situation has any relationship to another. They lack the ability to foresee consequences.

Implications

1. Give lots of affection, holding, cuddling, talking and listening. He is unable to understand rules, so correct his behavior with patience and love. He has a limited attention span. He will listen only to those things that interest him.

2. Provide short, vivid stories and games (peek-a-boo, patty-cake) that challenge his mental and sensory abilities. Provide repetition and practice short behaviors. Talk about Heavenly Father and Jesus and how to please them.

3. Do not try to teach concepts or rules; he cannot understand them. But do have rules and be consistent in applying them. Respond to him in positive ways to help him feel good about himself.

2 to 7 years of age

Characteristics

1. A child will display affection at odd moments. He may run to you for a quick hug and then go on with his play. He likes affection but only in brief doses. He may sometimes push unsought affection aside when his attention is elsewhere. He rejects your help even though there are many things he cannot do for himself, like drawing and other tasks requiring good finger and hand coordination.

2. A child may seem selfish, not sharing. He wants things others are using and does

not play with children so much as along side them. Disagreements and frustrations are common. He interrupts others and cannot stay long with one activity if others are not doing it. He likes stories and imitates others.

3. A child may seem willful and disobedient and unable to justify "naughty" behavior. His reasons may be illogical: "Jimmy (an imaginary friend) made me." He is often slow to obey and must be reminded.

Reasons

1. Parents meet most of a child's needs and satisfactions. As a child begins to conquer his world, he needs to know that this source of security is still there. He has an equally important need to do things, to be active, and to explore his world as his control over his body improves.

2. A child still thinks the world is the way he sees it, not understanding that there can be more than one reason for anything. He cannot understand others' needs. He cannot keep a lot of ideas in his head for very long, so he turns to other things when his attention lags or he gets bored.

3. "Good" means "satisfying" to him; he still doesn't understand that rules apply to many situations. He doesn't reason the same way adults do. He learns by testing the limits imposed upon him.

Implications

1. Give him simple things to do--holding pictures, leading songs. Increase these and add talks as he gets older. Let him feel he is an important part of family home evening. Give affection and praise. Practice "good" behaviors like folding arms and bowing heads, kneeling for prayers, drinking from a sacrament cup, and sitting still. Teach him about Jesus Christ and the gospel and how you feel about them.

3. Read or tell scripture stories. Explain the "hard" parts. Choose stories that give "good" behavior to copy. Explain in concrete terms, not in abstract principles. Define gospel words like repentance, faith, and forgiveness with familiar examples. Use examples, simply told, from your own or other family members' lives.

3.Introduce rules but keep them simple. Be firm and consistent. Help your child to be successful so he can develop self-confidence. Show how obedience will help him grow.

7 to 12 years of age

Characteristics

1. Boys may appear less open to affection than girls, particularly around others, but may accept it more willingly when hurt or frustrated. Both are active, like games, and prefer the company of their own sex.
2. They like games and may spend much time discussing rules, fairness, and cheating. Some are aggressive while others lack self-confidence. In school, girls may be more successful, obedient, and more interested than boys. A child might be interested in clubs, cliques, or neighborhood gangs, seeking friends outside the home.
3. He questions parents' decisions, wanting to know "why." When your explanations are fair or logical, he will accept them; if arbitrary or inconsistent, he will question them, but usually obey.

Reasons

1. Boys and girls are learning what they are all about. They play at the roles set for them much of the time. Although they look to each other for examples, parental love and approval are very important.
2. Games and clubs help the child learn about himself and how rules apply to his life. He is very aware of competition and concerned about his performance. Because girls are usually more adept at language and social skills at this age, they may do better than boys who may feel inferior or rejected.
2. A child has discovered that things that happen are governed by or explained by rules. Knowing the rules and how they apply is extremely important because it helps him predict consequences.

Implications

1. Be ready to listen. Give each child some personal time. Support your child in his problems. Provide real-life examples (stories and short examples) of good role models.
2. Provide challenging games that teach sportsmanship, honesty, and cooperation. Help boys get ready for priesthood service. Teach the commandments and obligations as children of our Father in Heaven. Choose activities that build family unity.
3. If your child questions decisions, do not become angry. Explain and then allow him to respond. Be fair and impartial in applying rules, helping him understand how Heavenly Father's rules are for our good.

11 to adulthood

Characteristics

1. A boy may become awkward and clumsy, while a girl may become silly and self-centered. Both may seem irresponsible.
2. Youth may enjoy sports, group activities, and discussions about "life," values, and principles (justice, equality, peace). But they may show great intolerance for others' opinions. They may want to escape the family but be afraid to do so.
3. Youth often question values and come to distrust rules, especially rules without any strong ethical or moral basis. They may insist upon their "rights" to be independent. They may seem uncertain of what is meant by "right" and "wrong" for a time. They often reject authority as a reason to approve or disapprove of a behavior.

Reasons

1. Physical growth and changes are emotionally upsetting; the youth feels that things are happening faster than he is ready for them. He feels more socially than physically

awkward.

2. Sports and play are no longer ways of exploring rules. They reassure youth about their abilities as they watch and copy others while establishing their own adult identities. Youth are especially concerned about relationships with each other. They may be insecure and uncertain about what society expects.

3. Youth have found by now that rules are not infallible. They are now able to handle abstract concepts and are busy building their own guiding philosophy of life. They now look behind the rules for the principles.

Implications

1. Discuss gospel and life principles with your child. Avoid arguing over his different views; rather teach by sharing your own faith, experiences, uncertainty. Be supportive, encouraging, and accepting. Be consistent in applying rules and explain them in terms of principles.

2. Encourage family support for your children's activities. Be friendly and open to their friends. Discuss marriage goals and how priesthood and service activities express the principles of love, brotherhood, and forgiveness. Find ways to bring their friends into family activities rather than competing for time and loyalty.

3. Teach the idea of baptism, priesthood, and marriage covenants. Help your children see scripture as a record of people trying to cope with problems. Give them opportunities to become involved in challenging discussions of ethical problems and gospel applications. These discussions are practice for making decisions on their own later.

Chapter – II
Review Literature

Akemi Tomoda, Teruhisa Miike, Noritaka Iwatani, Toshiro Ninomiya, Hiroyo Mabe, Toshiro Kageshita, Shosuke Ito (*November 1999*) Effect of long-term melatonin administration on school-phobic children and adolescents with sleep disturbances. Melatonin is effective in treating sleep disturbances, which are closely related to school phobia. However, side effects of melatonin in long-term administration have not been examined fully. In the present study melatonin was administered to 30 patients with school phobia (18 females, 12 males; mean age, 14.8 years) who had no physical, psychiatric, or social problems, but had sleep disturbances. Patients were compared with 27 healthy, age-matched controls. No changes in serum 5-S-cysteinyldopa levels, human skin pigmentation, or the state of puberty were observed in either group. Melatonin appeared to lead to improvements in sleep disturbances.

Andres G. Viana, Brian Rabian, Deborah C. Beidel (*June 2008*) Self-report measures in the study of comorbidity in children and adolescents with social phobia: Research and clinical utility. We examined differences in self-reported anxiety and depression according to the number and pattern of *DSM-IV* comorbid diagnoses in 172 children and adolescents (mean age = 11.87, S.D. = 2.67; range = 7–17) with a primary diagnosis of social phobia. Three hypotheses were tested: (1) children with comorbid anxiety disorders would show significantly higher scores than children with social phobia-only on self-report measures, (2) self-report measures would significantly differentiate between children with social phobia and comorbid internalizing versus externalizing disorders, and (3) self-report measures would significantly differentiate children according to the type of anxiety comorbidities present. Multinomial logistic regressions showed that children with three anxiety disorders scored significantly higher than children with one and two diagnoses on two of three self-report measures used. Logistic regressions revealed that children's scores on measures did not differ according to the nature of the comorbid diagnoses (internalizing vs. externalizing). Finally, ROC curves showed that the MASC and the SPAI-C accurately classified children with additional diagnoses of SAD and GAD, respectively. The potential of self-report measures to further our understanding of childhood anxiety comorbidity and the clinical implications of their use to screen for comorbidity are discussed along with suggestions for further study.

Anthony C. Puliafico, Jonathan S. Comer, Philip C. Kendall (*March 2007*) Social Phobia in Youth: The Diagnostic Utility of Feared Social Situations. The present study evaluated the utility of parent- and child-reported social fears for reaching a diagnosis of social phobia in youth. The diagnostic utility of (a) the number of fears and (b) specific feared social situations was examined. The sample included 140 youth and their parents: youth diagnosed with social phobia ($n = 50$), youth diagnosed with generalized anxiety disorder or separation anxiety disorder but not social phobia ($n = 49$), and youth without an anxiety disorder ($n = 41$). Youth and their parents were interviewed separately using the Anxiety Disorders Interview Schedule for Children and Parents. Analyses indicate that a cut score of 4 parent-endorsed social fears optimally distinguished youth with and without social phobia. Analyses of child-reported fears did not identify a meaningful cut score. Conditional probability and odds ratio analyses indicated that several specific social fears have high diagnostic efficiency, and others were found to have limited diagnostic efficiency. Results are discussed with regard to informing diagnostic interviews and diagnostic systems for social phobia in youth.

Candice A. Alfano, Armando A. Pina, Ian K. Villalta, Deborah C. Beidel, Robert T. Ammerman, Lori E. Crosby (*September 2009*) Mediators and Moderators of Outcome in the Behavioral Treatment of Childhood Social Phobia. Objective The current study examined mediators and moderators of treatment response among children and adolescents (ages 7–17 years) with a primary diagnosis of social phobia. Method Participants were 88 youths participating in one of two randomized controlled treatment trials of Social Effectiveness Therapy for Children. Potential mediators included changes in observer-rated social skill and child-reported loneliness after 12 weeks of Social Effectiveness Therapy for Children. Age and depressive symptoms were examined as potential moderators. Results Loneliness scores and social effectiveness during a role-play task predicted changes in social anxiety and overall functioning at posttreatment. Changes in social anxiety were mediated by child-reported loneliness. Outcomes were not moderated by age or depressive symptoms. Conclusions Findings support the role of loneliness as an important mechanism of change during treatment for childhood social phobia.

Carol J. M. van Velzen, Paul M. G. Emmelkamp, Agnes Scholing (*July-August 2000*) Generalized Social Phobia Versus Avoidant Personality Disorder: Differences in Psychopathology, Personality Traits, and Social and Occupational Functioning. Four groups of patients with social phobia (SP) were compared with regard to psychopathologic characteristics, personality traits, and social and occupational functioning. Fifteen persons with discrete social phobia without any personality disorder (DSP), 28 persons with generalized social phobia (GSP) without any personality disorder, 24 persons with GSP with a single diagnosis of avoidant personality disorder (APD), and 23 persons with GSP with more than one PD were included in the present study. APD had higher levels of social phobic avoidance, depressive symptoms, neuroticism, introversion, and social and occupational impairment as compared with GSP. DSP was found to be the least severe condition. OPD was the most impaired on nearly all variables. Logistic regression analyses revealed that introversion and depressive symptoms were able to predict correctly the presence or absence of an APD in 85% of those with social phobia. These findings are discussed in the light of the severity continuum hypothesis of social phobia and APD and recommendations for future research are given.

CATHERINE MANCINI, MICHAEL VAN AMERINGEN, PETER SZATMARI, CHRISTINA FUGERE, MICHAEL BOYLE (*November 1996*) A High-Risk Pilot Study of the Children of Adults with Social Phobia. Objective Children of patients with social phobia were studied to estimate their rates of psychiatric disorder. Method Twenty-six social-phobic outpatients who had at least one child between the ages of 4 and 18 years participated in the study. Information was collected from parents on all 47 children and from the children between 12 and 18 years of age. Diagnoses in the children were made based on *DSM-III-R* and were done by a best-estimate method, using parent and child reports from a modified Anxiety Disorders Interview Schedule for Children, the Survey Diagnostic Instrument, the Current Self-Report Childhood Inhibition Scale, and the Alcohol Dependence Survey. Results Of the 47 children, 49% had at least one lifetime anxiety disorder diagnosis. The most common diagnoses were overanxious disorder (30%), social phobia (23%), and separation anxiety disorder (19%). Sixty-five percent had more than one anxiety disorder diagnosis. Lifetime major depression was found in 8.5% of the children. Parents whose children met criteria for an anxiety disorder had a greater mean number of comorbid diagnoses than did the parents of unaffected children. Conclusion This pilot study suggests that children of social-phobic parents may have increased rates of psychiatric disorder. Further studies incorporating a control group are needed.

CYNTHIA G. LAST, CHERI HANSEN, NATHALIE FRANCO (*April 1998*) Cognitive-Behavioral Treatment of School Phobia. Objective To conduct a controlled group outcome investigation of the efficacy of cognitive-behavioral treatment for school phobia. Method Fifty-six children with school phobia were randomly assigned to 12 weeks of cognitive-behavioral therapy or an attention-placebo control condition. Pre- and posttreatment school attendance, self-reported anxiety and depression, and diagnostic status were compared. Results Both the experimental and control treatments were equally effective at returning children to school. Both treatments also were effective in reducing children's anxiety and depressive symptoms. Follow-up revealed no differences between groups when the children reentered school the next school year. Conclusions Overall, results suggest that psychosocial treatments are effective at returning school-phobic children to school and that the highly structured cognitive-behavioral approach may not be superior to more traditional educational and supportive treatment methods. *J. Am. Acad.*

DEBORAH C. BEIDEL (*July 1991*) Social Phobia and Overanxious Disorder in School-Age Children. Epidemiological data indicate that, based on current diagnostic criteria, anxiety disorders are the most common childhood disorders. Furthermore, the comorbidity rate among the various diagnostic categories is quite high, and relatively little attention has been given to delineating the specific and distinct parameters of these disorders. The current study examined the characteristics of overanxious disorder and social phobia by comparing children who have these disorders to matched normal controls. The results indicated that children with social phobia could be differentiated from the other groups, based on self-report inventories, daily diary data, and a psychophysiological assessment. However, there were few variables that distinguished overanxious children. The results provide strong support for the diagnostic validity of social phobia in children but lesser support for overanxious disorder as currently defined.

DEBORAH C. BEIDEL, SAMUEL M. TURNER, FLOYD R. SALLEE, ROBERT T. AMMERMAN, LORI A. CROSBY, SANJEEV PATHAK (*December 2007*) SET-C Versus Fluoxetine in the Treatment of Childhood Social Phobia. To determine the efficacy of fluoxetine, pill placebo, and Social Effectiveness Therapy for Children (SET-C) for children and adolescents with social phobia. Method Youths ages 7 to 17 were randomly assigned to one of the treatment conditions. Outcome was evaluated using self-reports, parent ratings, independent evaluator ratings, and behavioral assessment. Results Both fluoxetine and SET-C were more efficacious than placebo in reducing social distress and behavioral avoidance and increasing general functioning. SET-C was superior to fluoxetine on each of these measures and was the only treatment superior to placebo in terms of improving social skills, decreasing anxiety in specific social interactions, and enhancing ratings of social competence. Furthermore, whereas fluoxetine appears to exert maximum effect by 8 weeks, SET-C provides continued improvement through week 12.

DEBORAH C. BEIDEL, SAMUEL M. TURNER, TRACY L. MORRIS (*June 1999*) Psychopathology of Childhood Social Phobia. To describe the clinical syndrome of social phobia in preadolescent children. Method Fifty children with *DSM-IV* social phobia were assessed with semistructured diagnostic interviews, self-report instruments, parental and teacher ratings, a behavioral assessment, and daily diary recordings. In addition, the behaviors of these children were compared with those of a sample of normal peers. Results Children with social phobia had a high level of general emotional over-responsiveness, social fear and inhibition, dysphoria, loneliness, and general tearfulness. Sixty percent suffered from a second, concurrent disorder. Socially distressing events occurred quite frequently and were accompanied by maladaptive coping behaviors. In addition, children with social phobia had significantly poorer social skills. There were few differences based on gender or race. Conclusions Children with social phobia suffer pervasive and serious functional impairment. In addition, the clinical presentation suggests specific avenues for psychosocial interventions.

Denise A. Chavira, Murray B. Stein, Vanessa L. Malcarne *(2002)* Scrutinizing the relationship between shyness and social phobia. The nature of the relationship between shyness and social phobia can be clarified by assessing rates of social phobia in highly shy and normative samples. In the present study, 2202 participants were screened and categorized on a shyness scale as highly shy (90th percentile) or "normatively" shy (40–60th percentile). The Composite International Diagnostic Interview and the Structured Clinical Interview for DSM-IV Axis II Personality Disorders (SCID-II; Avoidant Personality Disorder module) were used to assign clinical diagnoses. Approximately 49% of individuals in the highly shy group had a social phobia diagnosis compared to 18% in the normatively shy group. Significantly more generalized social phobia (36% vs. 4%) and avoidant personality disorder (14% vs. 4%) diagnoses were present in the highly shy group compared to the normatively shy group. Equal rates of nongeneralized social phobia (i.e., 14% vs. 14%) were present in the highly shy and the normatively shy comparison group. Findings suggest that shyness and social phobia (especially the generalized type) are related constructs but not completely synonymous; an individual can be extremely shy yet not have a social phobia diagnosis.

Dirk van West, Stephan Claes, José Sulon, Dirk Deboutte *(December 2008)* Hypothalamic-pituitary-adrenal reactivity in prepubertal children with social phobia. The aim of this study was to investigate whether a different pattern of HPA axis activity is found between children with social phobia (SP) and healthy control children. Methods A total of 50 prepubertal subjects (25 children with SP and 25 healthy control subjects) were studied. The effects of stress were studied by comparing cortisol responses to a psychosocial stressor, consisting of a public speaking task. Results Children with SP showed an elevated cortisol response to the psychosocial stressor as compared with healthy controls. Trait but not state anxiety levels are associated with higher HPA axis activity. Limitations Limited sample size. Conclusions The results indicate that a higher cortisol responsivity to stress may be a neurobiological marker for prepubertal children with SP. Directions for future research and clinical implications are discussed.

Donald L. Tasto (*November 1969*) Systematic desensitization, muscle relaxation and visual imagery in the counterconditioning of four-year-old phobic child. A four-year-old boy with a severe phobia for loud sudden noises was successfully treated with behavior modification utilizing muscle relaxation and *in vivo* conditioning in six sessions. The question of theoretical importance was whether muscle relaxation and systematic desensitization by imagining feared stimuli could successfully be employed to treat a phobia in a child this young. The literature does not, to the author's knowledge, contain any reports of the combined use of muscle relaxation and imagination of fear-producing stimuli for treating phobic children of such a young age.

Edward Hampe, Helen Noble, Lovick C. Miller, Curtis L. Barrett (*December 1973*) Phobic children one and two years posttreatment. Evaluated progress of 62 phobic children 1 and 2 yrs after termination of treatment or waiting period. 80% were either symptom free or significantly improved; only 7% still had a severe phobia. Successfully treated Ss tended to remain symptom free and to be free from other deviant behaviors as well. 60% of the failures at termination continued to receive treatment and most were symptom free 2 yrs later. After 2 yrs, the effects of the original psychotherapy and reciprocal inhibition therapy no longer were related to outcome. However, age, status at the end of treatment, and time were related to outcome. Results are discussed in terms of the nature of child phobia and implications for research.

Eric A. Storch, Carrie Masia-Warner, Heather C. Dent, Jonathan W. Roberti, Paige H. Fisher (*2004*) Psychometric evaluation of the Social Anxiety Scale for Adolescents and the Social Phobia and Anxiety Inventory for Children: construct validity and normative data. This study evaluated the psychometric properties of the Social Anxiety Scale for Adolescents (SAS-A) and Social Phobia and Anxiety Inventory for Children (SPAI-C) in a sample of 1147 adolescents aged 13–17 years. The fit indices of confirmatory factor analyses were comparable to those obtained in prior studies and supported the hypothesized models of the SAS-A and SPAI-C. The internal consistency was good and 12-month test–retest reliability modest for both measures. A significant, positive correlation was found between the SAS-A and SPAI-C, showing that these measures assess related, but relatively independent constructs of social anxiety and phobia. These findings support the use of the SAS-A and SPAI-C with adolescents.

GAIL A. BERNSTEIN, PEDER H. SVINGEN, BARRY D. GARFINKEL (*January 1990*) School Phobia: Patterns of Family Functioning. Seventy-six families of children with school phobia were evaluated with the Family Assessment Measure. Mothers and fathers, as separate groups, rated clinically significant dysfunction in the parent-child relationship in the areas of role performance and values and norms. There were no significant differences between intact and single-parent families on ratings of family dysfunction. There was significantly less family dysfunction as rated by mothers and by children if the child had a diagnosis of pure anxiety disorder compared to families of school phobic children in other diagnostic categories.

Giulio Perugi, Stefano Nassini, Cristina Socci, Michele Lenzi, Cristina Toni, Elisa Simonini, Hagop S. Akiskal (*August 1999*) Avoidant personality in social phobia and panic–agoraphobic disorder: a comparison. *Background:* Avoidant personality disorder (APD) is generally believed to be related to social phobia (SP), especially to generalized subtype. However, it has also been reported to be prevalent in panic disorder–agoraphobia (PDA). In the present investigation, we wished to explore whether APD in each of these disorders has discriminatory features. *Method:* We studied 71 SP and 119 PDA patients with state-of-the-art clinical instruments based on DSM-III-R. *Results:* The pattern of social avoidance in SP was more pervasive: it was characterized by a higher level of interpersonal sensitivity and greater severity, associated with psychopathology as well as a higher rate of Axis I comorbidity. By contrast, avoidance of non-routine situations characterized APD occurring in the setting of PDA. *Limitations:* Differences in inclusion criteria and comorbidity rates, as well as overlap between different operational disorders, may have influenced our findings. *Conclusion:* ADP is operationally broad, and 'avoidant' as a specifier of a personality type is insufficiently precise. ADP captures avoidant traits — which appear secondary to a core dimension such as interpersonal sensitivity — but is basically a heterogeneous condition influenced by the nature of comorbid Axis I disorders.

GRETA FRANCIS, CYNTHIA G. LAST, CYD C. STRAUSS (*November 1992*) Avoidant Disorder and Social Phobia in Children and Adolescents. The diagnoses of avoidant disorder and social phobia in children have received little research attention. Although *DSM-III-R* describes avoidant disorder and social phobia as distinct disorders, no empirical data are available to support this notion. The current study examined characteristics of avoidant disorder and social phobia by comparing outpatient youngsters with avoidant disorder, social phobia, and avoidant disorder plus social phobia on demographic variables and patterns of comorbidity. The psychiatric groups were compared with matched normal controls on symptom measures of depression and fear. Findings indicated that the three psychiatric groups were strikingly similar on all but one variable, age at intake. These findings question the notion of avoidant disorder and social phobia as distinct disorders in children and adolescents.

Heather M. Gallagher, Brian A. Rabian, Michael S. McCloskey (*2004*) A brief group cognitive-behavioral intervention for social phobia in childhood. Twenty-three preadolescent children (ages 8–11) meeting criteria for social phobia were randomly assigned to either a 3-week cognitive-behavioral group intervention or a wait-list control group. The intervention consisted of psychoeducation, cognitive strategies, and behavioral exposure. Outcome measures included diagnostic interview as well as parent and child report measures of anxiety and depression. Improvements were observed at posttest, with results stronger for parent report and interviewer ratings than for child self-report. At 3-week follow-up, children receiving the intervention demonstrated significant improvements on the majority of child, parent, and interviewer reports of social anxiety and related symptoms relative to wait-list participants. Preliminary support is provided for the utility of a brief intervention for preadolescent children with social phobia. Limitations and implications for future research are discussed.

HERBERT A. SCHREIER, JUDITH A. LIBOW (*July 1986*) Acute Phobic Hallucinations in Very Young Children. Acute hallucinations in children aged 2–6 is not a rare occurrence. Emerging at times of stress, they are associated with severe anxiety and phobic behavior. The hallucinations are almost always visual and/or tactile. Contrary to reports of hallucinations at other ages, they tend to occur in bright, independent children. They are self-limited, with the acute hallucinatory phase over in a matter of several days and a subacute phobic phase which may last from weeks to months. In all of our cases there was a return to normal functioning. Hallucinations in this age group appear to be a different phenomenon from those occurring in older children, which are more frequently associated with more serious illnesses. These need to be understood in a developmental framework, but current knowledge does not permit a thorough explanation.

IRWIN J. MANSDORF, ELLEN LUKENS (*March 1987*) Cognitive-Behavioral Psychotherapy for Separation Anxious Children Exhibiting School Phobia. Two children—a 10-year-old boy and a 12-year-old girl—who exhibited severe school phobia (nonattendance for 6 consecutive weeks before referral), participated in an intervention program based on a psychodynamically oriented cognitive approach. The children were "nonresponders" both to imipramine therapy and to enrollment in a program to combat depression. The six-step program included the assessment of (a) cognitive analysis of the child: (b) environmental analysis; and (c) cognitive analysis of the parents; followed by (d) cognitive self-instructing of children; (e) cognitive restructuring of parents; and (f) environmental restructuring. Both children improved rapidly: subject 1 returned to school by week 4; subject 2 by week 2. The authors' approach to combating school phobia is described; more rigid research designs to evaluate the program are suggested.

J Reich (*May 2000*) The relationship of social phobia to avoidant personality disorder: a proposal to reclassify avoidant personality disorder based on clinical empirical findings. In the DSM system social phobia and avoidant personality have been conceptualized as independent entities. Each had separate, if overlapping diagnostic criteria. The specific inclusion and exclusion criteria provided by DSM allowed empirical research to guide future revisions. This review evaluates the

115

empirical literature and evolution of the concepts of these diagnoses from DSM-III to DSM-IIR to DSM-IV. The empirical evidence leads us to the conclusion that there is no dividing line between social phobia and avoidant personality disorder. In addition to their being no dividing line diagnostically between the disorders, there appears to be no separation of the two by treatment techniques. This raises interesting questions about how we differentiate Axis I from Axis II disorders. Suggestions for revisions of the social phobia and avoidant personality disorder categories are given.

James A. Tahmisian, William T. McReynolds (*May 1971*) Use of parents as behavioral engineers in the treatment of a school-phobic girl. Reports a case study of a 13-yr-old school-phobic girl successfully treated by her parents with instrumental behavior-shaping treatment procedures. Excluding the therapist's initial assessment with the child and an unsuccessful attempt with systematic desensitization, total treatment time was 3 wk. and total time expenditure of the therapist was approximately 2 hr. 90 min. for instruction and training of the parents and 10 min. for each of 3 subsequent follow-up telephone calls.

Kathleen Ries Merikangas, Shelli Avenevoli, Suddhasatta Acharyya, Heping Zhang, Jules Angst (*January 2002*) The spectrum of social phobia in the zurich cohort study of young adults. Background: The goals of the present study are to describe the prevalence, risk factors, course, and impact of social phobia in a 15-year prospective longitudinal community study; and to examine an expanded conceptualization of social phobia with respect to clinical indicators of severity, as well as gender differences, personality traits, and stability over 15 years. Methods: The sample is a cohort of 591 young adults aged 18–19 from the general population of Zurich, Switzerland at study entry who have been followed to age 35. Results: Six percent of participants met lifetime criteria for social phobia at the diagnostic level, 12% at the subthreshold level, and 24% had social phobia symptoms alone. Women had higher lifetime rates of diagnostic and subthreshold-level social phobia, whereas there was an equal gender ratio of social phobia symptoms. There was a direct association between strictness of the diagnostic threshold and severity, such that work impairment, social impairment, treatment rate, medication use, and subjective distress decreased from the diagnostic to the symptom level. Similarly, family history of phobias, autonomic

116

lability, and comorbidity decreased across the spectrum. Although there was a substantial degree of longitudinal stability at each level of the spectrum, significant oscillation across levels suggests that the spectrum concept better characterizes the longitudinal course of social phobia. Conclusions: These findings demonstrate the utility of the social phobia spectrum. Application of the spectrum concept provides coverage of treated but undiagnosed cases of social phobia as well as those who vacillate across the diagnostic threshold over time.

KENNETH J. ZWIER, UMA RAO (*September 1994*) Buspirone Use in an Adolescent with Social Phobia and Mixed Personality Disorder (Cluster A Type). The use of buspirone for the treatment of social phobia has been reported in some adult patients; however, to the authors' knowledge, there are no reports of its use in adolescents with this disorder. Use of buspirone in children and adolescents with anxiety disorders is reviewed. An unusual case study is presented of a 16-year-old male patient with social phobia and a mixed personality disorder predominantly with schizotypal features, who responded well to an open trial of buspirone for anxiety and "soft" psychotic symptoms.

LISSETTE M. SAAVEDRA, WENDY K. SILVERMAN (*November 2002*) Case Study: Disgust and a Specific Phobia of Buttons. The role of disgust in childhood phobias has received limited attention in the psychiatric literature. Available studies suggest that attention to the emotion of disgust is optimal for reduction of phobic symptoms given that the interaction between fear and disgust has been found to maintain and even exacerbate phobias. Disgust was targeted via imagery exposures as part of an exposure-based cognitive-behavioral intervention for a 9-year-old Hispanic American boy who presented with a specific phobia of buttons. Posttreatment, 6-month, and 12-month follow-up assessment results demonstrated maintenance of treatment gains. The role of disgust in treating specific phobias in children is discussed.

Louise M. Dewis, Kenneth C. Kirkby, Frances Martin, Brett A. Daniels, Lisa J. Gilroy, Ross G. Menzies (*March 2001*) Computer-aided vicarious exposure versus live graded exposure for spider phobia in children. The efficacy of computer-aided

117

vicarious exposure (CAVE) for the treatment of spider phobia in children was evaluated in a single blind, randomised, controlled trial. Twenty-eight participants, aged 10–17 years, received three 45-min sessions of either Live graded exposure (LGE), CAVE or were assigned to a Waitlist. Phobic symptomatology was measured at pre- and post-treatment, and at one month follow-up on a range of behavioural and subjective assessments. The results showed the superiority of the LGE treatment over the CAVE and Waitlist conditions. Effect sizes support CAVE treatment as being superior to the Waitlist and resulting in reductions of phobic symptomatology.

LYNN T. SINGER, BRUCE AMBUEL, SHARI WADE, ARTHUR C. JAFFE *(September 1992)* Cognitive-Behavioral Treatment of Health-Impairing Food Phobias in Children. Three case reports describe assessment and treatment of three boys (ages 6 to 8 years) hospitalized because of weight loss and malnutrition, caused by severe dietary restriction and/or refusal to eat solid food. Psychological, behavioral, and medical assessments indicated that the boys were of average intelligence, without other significant psychological or medical disorders. Their eating disturbances were conceptualized as phobic disorders maintained by family factors reinforcing the children's avoidant behaviors. Cognitive-behavioral treatment consisted of an individualized combination of contingency management, shaping, desensitization, relaxation training, education, and cognitive restructuring. Generalization and maintenance were promoted by training parents to implement treatment at home before discharge. Treatment positively affected overall caloric intake, weight gain, number of solid foods accepted, and incidence of emesis.

M. Faytout, J. Tignol, J. Swendsen, D. Grabot, B. Aouizerate, J.P. Lépine *(March 2007)* Social phobia, fear of negative evaluation and harm avoidance. This naturalistic, prospective investigation examined the role of fear of negative evaluation and the personality trait of harm avoidance in the anxiety levels of treated social phobia patients. One hundred and fifty-seven patients with DSM-IV social phobia were assessed before starting treatment and were then followed for up to two years. As expected, greater fear of negative evaluation and higher scores of harm avoidance were associated with greater anxiety at the 6 month follow-up, and harm avoidance remained a significant predictor at 24 months. However, no evidence was found for an interaction between the personality and cognitive variables examined. The findings are discussed in terms of the relative independence of these factors, as well as their potential implications for the treatment of this disorder.

Maria Tillfors, Tomas Furmark, Lisa Ekselius, Mats Fredrikson (*March 2001*) Social phobia and avoidant personality disorder as related to parental history of social anxiety: a general population study. Using a validated and DSM-IV compatible questionnaire, the present study related family history of excessive social anxiety to social phobia and avoidant personality disorder (APD) in epidemiologically identified probands in the general population. Probands met diagnostic criteria for social phobia with or without APD and APD with or without social phobia. A two- to three-fold increased relative risk of social anxiety was observed for all diagnostic groups. Increasing severity in probands by varying diagnostic criteria did not affect the relative risk. Because familial aggregation of social anxiety was not modulated by Axis I or II diagnosis or diagnostic cut-off levels, data imply that social phobia and APD may represent a dimension of social anxiety rather than separate disorders. Thus, having an affected family member is associated with a two- to three-fold risk increase for both social phobia and APD.

Marteinsdottir, T. Furmark, M. Tillfors, M. Fredrikson, L. Ekselius (*April 2001*) Personality traits in social phobia. The purpose was to assess personality traits in subjects with a DSM-IV diagnosis of social phobia. Thirty-two subjects were administered the Structured Clinical Interview for DSM-IV for Axes I and II disorders (SCID I and II). Personality traits were assessed by means of the Karolinska Scales of Personality (KSP). Current and lifetime axis I co-morbidity was diagnosed in 28% and 53% of the subjects, respectively. In total, 59% had at least one personality disorder and 47% were diagnosed with an avoidant personality disorder. The social phobics scored significantly higher than a Swedish normative sample on the KSP measuring anxiety proneness, irritability, detachment, and indirect aggression but lower on the scales for socialisation and social desirability. The presence as compared to absence of avoidant personality disorder in the social phobics was associated with significantly higher psychic anxiety and inhibition of aggression. In addition, symptom severity was higher in social phobics with an avoidant personality disorder.

Generally, the results support the view that social phobia and avoidant personality disorder reflect different aspects of a social anxiety spectrum.

Martin L. Boone, Daniel W. McNeil, Carrie L. Masia, Cynthia L. Turk, Leslie E. Carter, Barry J. Ries, Michael R. Lewin (*May 1999*) Multimodal Comparisons of Social Phobia Subtypes and Avoidant Personality Disorder. The purpose of the present study was to further clarify the behavioral, physiological, and verbal response of patients with circumscribed social (speech) phobia, generalized social phobia without avoidant personality disorder, and generalized social phobia with avoidant personality disorder. Patients completed a battery of verbal report instruments and participated in two behavioral assessment tests. Measures of avoidance/escape behavior, cardiac response, level of behavioral skill, state anxiety, and positive and negative self-statements during performance were collected. Significant differences across response domains were found between the circumscribed social phobia and the generalized groups. Most of the distinctions were between individuals with circumscribed social phobia and those with both generalized social phobia and avoidant personality disorder, with the former group having less overall psychopathology. In addition, there was substantial overlap of problems between generalized social phobia individuals with and without avoidant personality disorder. Implications for the conceptualization of social phobia are discussed in terms of the differences among social phobia subtypes.

Martin Obler, Robert F. Terwilliger (*June 1970*) Pilot study on the effectiveness of systematic desensitization with neurologically impaired children with phobic disorders. A modified version of J. Wolpe's systematic desensitization therapy involving direct confrontation with the fear-inducing stimulus was attempted with 30 neurologically impaired children with phobic symptoms. 2 hypotheses were tested: (a) a nonverbal therapeutic technique not requiring motivation will produce successful symptom reduction for these Ss, and (b) awareness of therapeutic procedure is not necessary for successful results. Both hypotheses were confirmed.

Mauro V. Mendlowicz, Raphael J. Braga, Mariana Cabizuca, Marcelo G. Land, Ivan L. Figueira (*November 2006*) A comparison of publication trends on avoidant personality disorder and social phobia. The objective of this study was to ascertain the number of articles published per annum on the topics of avoidant personality disorder (APD) and social phobia (SP) in the period from 1973 to 2001. We hypothesized that while annual publication rates on SP would exhibit a sound growth, the number of scientific articles on APD published per annum would present a stagnant or declining trend. We performed a comprehensive literature review on APD and SP using the three largest existing databases for medical and psychological journals: MEDLINE, PsycINFO, and Web of Science. The references were gathered by means of the Reference Manager version 9.5 software and transferred to an SPSS version 10 database for statistical analysis. The data were then input into regression models with the goal of predicting future growth of the scientific literature in these areas. The number of journal articles published annually on SP has steadily increased in the period from 1973 (1 article) to 2001 (118 articles). In contrast, the production of scientific literature on APD peaked in 1986 (5 articles) and subsequently declined. During the last decade reviewed, an average of fewer than two articles on APD was published per annum. Given the declining trend identified in this study, we believe that it is unlikely that the publication of scientific articles on APD will provide the empirical evidence required to validate this disorder in a foreseeable future. The permanence of APD on the rolls of the personality disorders should therefore be reassessed.

Michael C. Ashton, Kibeom Lee, Beth A. Visser, Julie A. Pozzebon (*June 2008*) Phobic tendency within the Five-Factor and HEXACO models of personality structure. Recent research has indicated that the various specific phobias are only modestly correlated with the personality dimensions of the Big Five or Five-Factor Model (B5/FFM). We tested the hypothesis that the specific phobias would be more strongly associated with the dimensions of an alternative framework, the HEXACO model of personality structure. Self-reports on the Phobic Stimuli Response Scales (PSRS) were obtained along with self- and peer reports on measures of the B5/FFM and HEXACO dimensions from a sample of 248 non-clinical participants. The PSRS variables assessing specific phobias showed stronger correlations with the HEXACO Emotionality factor than with any B5/FFM dimension, and a stronger multiple correlation with the HEXACO factors than with the B5/FFM dimensions. Findings were similar across self- and peer reports of the personality variables. The results suggest that phobic tendency can be understood in terms of normal personality variation as conceptualized in the HEXACO framework.

O. Joseph Bienvenu, Clayton Brown, Jack F. Samuels, Kung-Yee Liang, Paul T. Costa, William W. Eaton, Gerald Nestadt (*May 2001*) Normal personality traits and comorbidity among phobic, panic and major depressive disorders. High comorbidity among anxiety and depressive conditions is a consistent but not well-understood finding. The current study examines how normal personality traits relate to this comorbidity. In the Baltimore Epidemiologic Catchment Area Follow-up Study, psychiatrists administered the full Schedules for Clinical Assessment in Neuropsychiatry to 320 subjects, all of whom completed the Revised NEO Personality Inventory. The disorders of interest were simple phobia, social phobia, agoraphobia, panic disorder, and major depression. Analyses were carried out with second-order generalized estimating equations. The unadjusted summary odds ratio (SOR — or weighted mean odds ratio) for all five disorders was 1.72 (95% confidence INTERVAL=1.21–2.46). Neuroticism, introversion, younger age, and female gender were all significant predictors of prevalence of disorders. After adjustment for the relationships between these personality and demographic predictors and prevalence, the association among disorders was much weaker (SOR=1.11, 95% CI=0.79–1.56). However, subjects with high extraversion had a SOR 213% as high (95% CI=102–444%) as those with low extraversion (1.60 vs. 0.75). Therefore, neuroticism and introversion are associated with increased comorbidity due to relationships in common with the prevalence of the different disorders. In contrast, extraversion is associated with increased comorbidity per se.

Peter Muris, Harald Merckelbach, Peter J. de Jong, Thomas H. Ollendick (*February 2002*) The etiology of specific fears and phobias in children: a critique of the non-associative account. The non-associative account of phobic etiology assumes that a number of specific fears (e.g., fear of heights, water, spiders, strangers, and separation) have an evolutionary background and may occur in the absence of learning experiences (e.g., conditioning). By this view, these specific fears pertain to stimuli that once posed a challenge to the survival of our prehistoric ancestors.

Accordingly, they would emerge spontaneously during the course of normal development and only in a minority of individuals, these specific fears would persist into adulthood. While the non-associative approach has generated interesting findings, several critical points can be raised. First, it capitalizes on negative findings, i.e., the failure to document learning experiences (e.g., conditioning, modeling) in the history of phobic children. Second, it largely ignores factors that have been found to be crucial for the acquisition of early childhood fears (e.g., the developmental level of the child, stimulus characteristics such as novelty, aversiveness, and unpredictability, and early experience with uncontrollable events). As an alternative to the non-associative account, we briefly describe a multifactorial model of childhood fears and phobias.

Peter Muris, Henk Schmidt, Harald Merckelbach *(September 1999)* The structure of specific phobia symptoms among children and adolescents. Previous research [Frederikson, M., Annas, P., Fisher, H. & Wik, G. (1996). Gender and age differences in the prevalence of specific fears and phobias. *Behaviour Research and Therapy, 34*, 33–39.] has shown that specific phobia symptoms of adults cluster into three subtypes: animal phobia, blood-injection-injury phobia and environmental–situational phobia. The present study examined whether these specific phobia subtypes can also be found in children. 996 children aged between 7 and 19 years completed a brief questionnaire regarding the frequency with which they experienced specific phobia symptoms. Confirmatory factor analysis was employed to examine the structure of these data. Results showed that childhood specific phobia symptoms indeed cluster into the three subtypes as described by Frederikson et al. and that these subtypes are either intercorrelated or the product of a single higher order factor. This structure appeared to be largely invariant across genders and age groups.

ROBIN YEGANEH, DEBORAH C. BEIDEL, SAMUEL M. TURNER, ARMANDO A. PINA, WENDY K. SILVERMAN *(September 2003)* Clinical Distinctions Between Selective Mutism and Social Phobia: An Investigation of Childhood Psychopathology. Objective To investigate the hypothesis that children with selective mutism are more socially anxious than children with social anxiety disorder but who are not selectively mute. Method Twenty-three children with comorbid selective mutism and social phobia and 23 age-matched controls with social phobia alone and their parents participated in a comprehensive assessment of social anxiety and related aspects of psychopathology. Results The results do not uniformly support previous suggestions that children with selective mutism refuse speech because they are "frozen with fear." Although clinician and observer ratings for children with selective mutism revealed higher ratings of social distress than for children with social phobia alone, self-report data do not support this conclusion. Furthermore, although there were no group differences on measures of trait anxiety, general fears, or scores on the Child Behavior Checklist broadband Internalizing or Externalizing scales, children with selective mutism scored higher than children with social phobia alone on the Child Behavior Checklist Delinquency subscale, suggesting the presence of a broader clinical syndrome. Conclusion It remains unclear whether children with selective mutism have extreme levels of social anxiety. Potential areas that might shed further light on this interesting disorder are discussed.

SCOTT N. COMPTON, AIMEE H. NELSON, JOHN S. MARCH (*August 2000*) Social Phobia and Separation Anxiety Symptoms in Community and Clinical Samples of Children and Adolescents. To examine the developmental progression and pattern of self-reported symptoms of social phobia (SP) and separation anxiety (SA) in community ($n = 2,384$) and clinical ($n = 217$) samples of children and adolescents, using a cross-sectional method. Method Subjects were cross-classified by age, gender, and race. Using mean scores on the SP and SA subscales of the Multidimensional Anxiety Scale for Children, 4 categories of children were established: HighSP/HighSA, HighSP/LowSA, LowSP/HighSA, and LowSP/LowSA. Data were analyzed using a generalized logit model. Results *Community sample:* Preadolescents and females reported more symptoms of HighSP/HighSA and LowSP/HighSA than adolescents and males. White children reported more symptoms of HighSP/LowSA, while the opposite pattern was found among African-American children. *Clinical sample:* Similar to the community sample, preadolescents reported more symptoms of HighSP/HighSA. However, clinical males reported more symptoms of LowSP/HighSA than clinical females. Conclusions In general, adolescents endorsed more symptoms of SP and fewer symptoms of SA than preadolescent children. Irrespective of age, white children endorsed more symptoms of SP and fewer symptoms of SA than African-American children. In the community sample, preadolescent boys endorsed more symptoms of SA and fewer symptoms of SP, suggesting a possible referral bias.

Soo-Jin Kim, Bung-Nyun Kim, Soo-Churl Cho, Jae-Won Kim, Min-Sup Shin, Hee-Jung Yoo, Hyo Won Kim (*August 2010*) The prevalence of specific phobia and associated co-morbid features in children and adolescents. The aims of this study were to investigate the prevalence, associated co-morbid psychiatric disorders and behavioral/emotional problems associated with the subtypes of specific phobia in children and adolescents. Methods A total of 2673 randomly selected children and adolescents from Seoul, Korea were assessed using the parent version of the Diagnostic Interview Schedule for Children (DISC-IV) and Children's Behavior Checklist (CBCL). We analyzed differences in psychiatric co-morbidities and CBCL profiles among the subtypes of specific phobia. ResultsThe 1-year prevalence of specific phobia was 7.9% (95% CI 7.63–8.17). Animal phobia was associated with anxiety disorder (OR 8.68, 95% CI 1.91–39.51) and oppositional defiant disorder (OR 2.55, 95% CI 1.27–5.12). Nature–environment phobia was associated with anxiety disorder (OR 25.70, 95% CI 6.16–107.10). Blood–injection–injury phobia showed associations with attention-deficit/hyperactivity disorder (ADHD: OR 6.74, 95% CI 2.81–16.15). Subjects with nature–environment phobia scored higher than did controls on the anxious/depressed, social problems, attention problems, and total behavioral problem profiles of the CBCL. Subjects with blood–injection–injury phobia scored significantly higher than did controls on the attention problems, aggressive behaviors, and externalizing problem profiles. Conclusions Contrary to animal phobias, nature–environment and blood–injection–injury phobias were associated with various behavioral and emotional problems and approximately correlated to their co-morbid psychiatric disorders. Among these subtypes, significant differences were found in demographic characteristics, co-morbid psychiatric disorders, and emotional/behavioral problems. These findings suggest that distinctive clinical characteristics might be related with different subtypes of specific phobia and clinician must consider psychiatric co-morbidities when treating children & adolescents with specific phobia.

SUSAN BAER, E JANE GARLAND (*March 2005*) Pilot Study of Community-Based Cognitive Behavioral Group Therapy for Adolescents With Social Phobia) Objective: A pilot study to evaluate the efficacy of a cognitive-behavioral group therapy program for adolescents with social phobia, simplified both in terms of time and labor intensity from a previously studied program (Social Effectiveness Therapy for Children and Adolescents) to be more appropriate for a community outpatient psychiatric setting. Method: Twelve adolescents with social phobia (ages 13-18), diagnosed by *DSM-IV* criteria and confirmed with Anxiety Disorders Interview Schedule for Children assessment, were randomly assigned to treatment (*n* = 6) and waitlist (*n* = 6) groups. The waitlist group was subsequently treated, and results were included in the data analysis. Assessments, including Anxiety Disorders Interview Schedule for Children interviews and self-report Social Phobia and Anxiety Inventory and Beck Depression Inventory II questionnaires, were performed at baseline and immediately after treatment or waitlist. Results: All subjects completed the treatment program. Compared with the waitlist group, treated subjects showed significantly greater improvement in both examiner-evaluated (Anxiety Disorders Interview Schedule for Children) and self-reported (Social Phobia and Anxiety Inventory) symptoms of social anxiety (effect sizes [d], 1.63 and 0.85, respectively). No significant change was seen in Beck Depression Inventory II scores for treatment or waitlist groups. Conclusions: This study provides support for the use of simplified cognitive-behavioral interventions for adolescents with social phobia that are practical for community psychiatric settings.

Thomas H. Ollendick, Lars-Göran Öst, Lena Reuterskiöld, Natalie Costa, Rio Cederlund, Cristian Sirbu, Thompson E. Davis III, Matthew A. Jarrett (*June 2009*) One-Session Treatment of Specific Phobias in Youth: A Randomized Clinical Trial in the United States and Sweden. One hundred and ninety-six youth, ages 7–16, who fulfilled *Diagnostic and Statistical Manual of Mental Disorders* (4th ed.) criteria for various specific phobias were randomized to a one-session exposure treatment, education support treatment, or a wait list control group. After the waiting period, the wait list participants were offered treatment and, if interested, rerandomized to 1 of the 2 active treatments. The phobias were assessed with semistructured diagnostic interviews, clinician severity ratings, and behavioral avoidance tests, whereas fears, general anxiety, depression, and behavior problems were assessed with self- and parent report measures. Assessments were completed pretreatment, posttreatment, and at 6 months following treatment. Results showed that both treatment conditions were superior to the wait list control condition and that 1-session exposure treatment was superior to education support treatment on clinician ratings of phobic severity, percentage of participants who were diagnosis free, child ratings of anxiety during the behavioral avoidance test, and treatment satisfaction as reported by the youth and their parents. There were no differences on self-report measures. Treatment effects were maintained at follow-up. Implications of these findings are discussed.

Thompson E. Davis III, Anna May, Sara E. Whiting *(June 2011)* Evidence-based treatment of anxiety and phobia in children and adolescents: Current status and effects on the emotional response. Research on treatments for childhood anxiety disorders has increased greatly in recent decades. As a result, it has become increasingly necessary to synthesize the findings of these treatment studies into reviews in order to draw wider conclusions on the efficacy of treatments for childhood anxiety. Previous reviews of this literature have used varying criteria to determine the evidence base. For the current review, stricter criteria consistent with the original Task Force (1995) guidelines were used to select and evaluate studies. Studies were divided by anxiety disorder; however, many studies combine various anxiety disorders in their samples. As a result, these were included in a combined anxiety disorder group. Using more traditional guidelines, studies were assigned a status of well-established, probably efficacious, or experimental based on the available literature and the quality of the studies. While some treatments do meet the criteria for well-established status, it is clear from this examination that gaps remain and replication is necessary to establish many of these treatments as efficacious. In addition, there still appears to be a lack of research on the effects of treatment on the physiological and cognitive aspects of fear and anxiety.

Thompson E. Davis III, Patricia F. Kurtz, Andrew W. Gardner, Nicole B. Carman *(November-December 2007)* Cognitive-behavioral treatment for specific phobias with a child demonstrating severe problem behavior and developmental delays. Cognitive-behavioral treatments (CBTs) are widely used for anxiety disorders in typically developing children; however, there has been no previous attempt to administer CBT for specific phobia (in this case study, one-session treatment) to developmentally or intellectually disabled children. This case study integrates both cognitive-behavioral and behavior analytic assessment techniques in the CBT of water and height phobia in a 7-year-old male with developmental delays and severe behavior problems. One-session treatment [Öst, L. G. (1989). One-session treatment for specific phobias. *Behaviour Research and Therapy*, *27*, 1–7; Öst, L. G. (1997). Rapid treatment of specific phobias. In G. C. L. Davey (Ed.), *Phobias: A handbook of theory, research, and treatment* (pp. 227–247). New York: Wiley] was provided for water phobia and then 2 months later for height phobia. The massed exposure therapy sessions combined graduated in vivo exposure, participant modeling, cognitive challenges, reinforcement, and other techniques. Both indirect and direct observation measures were utilized to evaluate treatment efficacy. Results suggested CBT reduced or eliminated behavioral avoidance, specific phobia symptoms, and subjective fear. Negative vocalizations were reduced during height exposure following treatment. Vocalizations following treatment for water phobia were less clear and may have been indicative of typical 7-year-old protests during bath time. Findings indicate CBT can be effective for treating clinical fears in an individual with developmental disabilities and severe behavior. Future research in this population should examine CBT as an alternative to other techniques (e.g., forced exposure) for treating fears.

Tina In-Albon, Kathrin Dubi, Ronald M. Rapee, Silvia Schneider (*December 2009*) Forced choice reaction time paradigm in children with separation anxiety disorder, social phobia, and nonanxious controls. Cognitive distortions refer to cognitive processes that are biased and therefore yield dysfunctional and maladaptive products (e.g., interpretation bias). Automatic aspects of information processing need to be considered and investigating these aspects requires forms of assessment other than self-report. Studies focussing on the specificity of cognitive biases across different types of anxiety disorders in childhood are rare. Thus, a forced choice reaction time paradigm with picture stimuli was used to assess the interpretation bias in anxious children online. The study investigated disorder-specific interpretation bias in 71 children with separation anxiety disorder (SAD), 31 children with social phobia, and 42 children without mental disorders, aged 5–13 years. Results indicated that children with SAD rated ambiguous separation pictures as significantly more unpleasant and more arousing than nonanxious children. However, no support was found that children with SAD and social phobia interpret ambiguous separation or social pictures in a more negative way than nonanxious children. Furthermore, no group differences were found in reaction times to all picture categories.

Tore Aune, Tore C. Stiles, Kyrre Svarva (*August 2008*) Psychometric properties of the Social Phobia and Anxiety Inventory for Children using a non-American population-based sample. Although previous studies have examined the factor structure of the SPAI-C, adequate factor analytic methodology has not been employed. This study explored the psychometric properties of the Social Phobia and Anxiety Inventory for Children (SPAI-C), using a non-American population-based sample of older children and young adolescents 11–14 years of age. Initially an exploratory factor analysis was conducted followed 1 year later by a confirmatory factor analysis. Five factors labeled *Assertiveness*, *Public Performance*, *Physical/Cognitive Symptoms*, *Social Encounter*, and *Avoidance* were retained and confirmed. The *Public Performance* and *Assertiveness* factors were the most stable and consistent factors or traits of social anxiety over a 1-year period. Results revealed adequate concurrent validity, internal consistency and moderate 12-month test–retest reliability of the SPAI-C total scale. The SPAI-C was found to assess levels of both social anxiety and social anxiety disorder according to DSM-IV criteria. Findings suggest that the SPAI-C is applicable in clinical treatment studies designed to assess sensitivity to change in various aspects of social anxiety disorder.

Verena Leutgeb, Axel Schäfer, Angelika Köchel, Wilfried Scharmüller, Anne Schienle (*December 2010*) Psychophysiology of spider phobia in 8- to 12-year-old girls. The present investigation focused on late event-related potentials (ERPs) and facial electromyographic (EMG) activity in response to symptom provocation in 8- to 12-year-old spider phobic girls and compared results to those in non-fearful controls. Fourteen patients and 14 controls were presented with phobia-relevant, generally fear-inducing, disgust-inducing and affectively neutral pictures in an EEG/EMG session. ERPs were extracted in the time-windows 340–500 ms (P300) and 550–770 ms (late positive potential, LPP). Relative to controls, phobics showed enhanced amplitudes of

P300 and LPP in response to spider pictures. This result is interpreted to reflect motivated attention to emotionally salient stimuli. Moreover, phobics showed enhanced average facial EMG activity of the levator labii and the corrugator supercilii in response to spider pictures, reflecting the negative valence and disgust relevance of spiders. Additionally, spider phobic girls relative to controls showed higher overall disgust proneness and heightened average facial EMG activity in both muscle regions in response to disgust stimuli, possibly revealing a disgust-based origin of spider phobia in children. These aspects should be considered in psychotherapeutic treatment of childhood spider phobia.

Wendy K. Silverman, Golda S. Ginsburg, William M. Kurtines (*Summer 1995*) Clinical issues in treating children with anxiety and phobic disorders. Issues involved in conducting cognitive behavioral treatment with children who present with anxiety and phobic disorders are discussed. The rationale for using cognitive behavioral treatment procedures is based on our premise that effective, long-term child behavior change depends on an adequate "transfer of control" from therapist to parent to child. The treatment involves separate and conjoint child and parent sessions and is implemented in three phases: education, application, and relapse prevention. Specific treatment strategies, common obstacles to implementing these strategies, and suggestions to address these obstacles are described for each phase of the treatment. A case vignette illustrates some of the treatment issues discussed.

Chapter – III
Methodology

Phobic disorders are common disorders that typically have their onset in childhood or adolescence. They are unique among psychiatric disorders in that the main categories of phobias are distinguished by the nature of an external stimulus rather than by differences in symptoms or course. Thus, individuals who have an irrational fear of animals are diagnosed with specific phobia, whereas those fear is triggered by people are diagnosed with social phobia. However, the quality of each disorder is distinctive. For example, generalized social phobia is often a chronic condition whose effects can be so pervasive and enduring that they seem to merge inextricably with underlying personality.

Aim of the Study:

The present study aimed at to study the strength of association between personality & phobic reaction, and find out the effect of type of family, sex, & birth order on personality of children.

Objectives of the Study:

1. To examine the Correlation in between Personality and Phobic Reaction of school going Ss.

2. To examine the Decisiveness among Joint Family and Nuclear Family school going Ss.

3. To examine the Decisiveness among Male and Female school going Ss.

4. To examine the Decisiveness among first Born and Last Born school going Ss.

5. To examine the Responsibility among Joint Family and Nuclear Family school going Ss.

6. To examine the Responsibility among Male and Female school going Ss.

7. To examine the Responsibility among first Born and Last Born school going Ss.

8. To examine the Emotional Stability among Joint Family and Nuclear Family school going Ss.

131

9. To examine the Emotional Stability among Male and Female school going Ss.

10. To examine the Emotional Stability among first Born and Last Born school going Ss.

11. To examine the Masculinity among Joint Family and Nuclear Family school going Ss.

12. To examine the Masculinity among Male and Female school going Ss.

13. To examine the Masculinity among first Born and Last Born school going Ss.

14. To examine the Friendliness among Joint Family and Nuclear Family school going Ss.

15. To examine the Friendliness among Male and Female school going Ss.

16. To examine the Friendliness among first Born and Last Born school going Ss.

17. To examine the Heterosexuality among Joint Family and Nuclear Family school going Ss.

18. To examine the Heterosexuality among Male and Female school going Ss.

19. To examine the Heterosexuality among first Born and Last Born school going Ss.

20. To examine the Ego Strength among Joint Family and Nuclear Family school going Ss.

21. To examine the Ego Strength among Male and Female school going Ss.

22. To examine the Ego Strength among first Born and Last Born school going Ss.

23. To examine the Curiosity among Joint Family and Nuclear Family school going Ss.

24. To examine the Curiosity among Male and Female school going Ss.

25. To examine the Curiosity among first Born and Last Born school going Ss.

26. To examine the Dominance among Joint Family and Nuclear Family school going Ss.

27. To examine the Dominance among Male and Female school going Ss.

28. To examine the Dominance among first Born and Last Born school going Ss.

29. To examine the Phobic Reaction among Joint Family and Nuclear Family school going Ss.

30. To examine the Phobic Reaction among Male and Female school going Ss.

31. To examine the Phobic Reaction among first Born and Last Born school going Ss.

Hypothesis:

1. Correlation in between Decisiveness and Phobic Reaction of school going Ss will be negative.

2. There will be negative Correlation in between Responsibility and Phobic Reaction of school going Ss.

3. The relationship between Emotional Stability and Phobic Reaction of school going Ss will be negative.

4. Correlation in between Masculinity and Phobic Reaction of school going Ss will be insignificant.

5. There will be negative Correlation in between Friendliness and Phobic Reaction of school going Ss.

6. Correlation in between Heterosexuality and Phobic Reaction of school going Ss will be non significant.

7. There will be negative Correlation in between Ego strength and Phobic Reaction of school going Ss.

8. The relationship between Curiosity and Phobic Reaction of school going Ss will be negative.

9. Correlation between Dominance and Phobic Reaction of school going Ss will be non significant.

10. The Ss coming from Joint family have significantly high Decisiveness than the Ss coming from Nuclear family.

11. Male Ss have significantly high Decisiveness than the Female Ss.

12. First born Ss have significantly high Decisiveness than the Last born school going Ss.

13. Ss coming from joint family have significantly high Responsibility than the Ss coming from nuclear family.

14. Male Ss have significantly high Responsibility than the Female Ss.

15. First born school going Ss have significantly high Responsibility than the Last born school going Ss.

16. Joint family school going Ss have significantly high Emotional Stability than Nuclear family school going Ss.

17. Male school going Ss have significantly high Emotional Stability than the Female school going Ss.

18. First born school going Ss have significantly high Emotional Stability than the Last born school going Ss.

19. Joint family school going Ss have significantly high Masculinity than the Nuclear family school going Ss.

20. Male school going Ss have significantly high Masculinity than the Female school going Ss.

21. First born school going Ss have significantly high Masculinity than the Last born school going Ss.

22. Joint family school going Ss have significantly high Friendliness than the Nuclear family school going Ss.

23. Male school going Ss have significantly high Friendliness than the Female school going Ss.

24. First born school going Ss have significantly high Friendliness than the Last born school going Ss.

25. Joint family school going Ss have significantly high Heterosexuality than the Nuclear family school going Ss.

26. Male school going Ss have significantly high Heterosexuality than the Female school going Ss.

27. First born school going Ss have significantly high Heterosexuality than the Last born school going Ss.

28. Joint family school going Ss have significantly high Ego Strength than the Nuclear family school going Ss.

29. Male school going Ss have significantly high Ego Strength than the Female school going Ss.

30. First born school going Ss have significantly high Ego Strength than the Last born school going Ss.

31. Joint family school going Ss have significantly high Curiosity than the Nuclear family school going Ss.

32. Male school going Ss have significantly high Curiosity than the Female school going Ss.

33. First born school going Ss have significantly high Curiosity than the Last born school going Ss.

34. Joint family school going Ss have significantly high Dominance than the Nuclear family school going Ss.

35. Male school going Ss have significantly high Dominance than the Female school going Ss.

36. First born school going Ss have significantly high Dominance than the Last born school going Ss.

37. Joint family school going Ss shows significantly high Phobic Reaction than the Nuclear family school going Ss.

38. Female school going Ss shows significantly high Phobic Reaction than the male school going Ss.

39. First born school going Ss shows significantly high Phobic Reaction than the Last born school going Ss.

Sample:

> After carefully studying location of the high schools, 10 high schools were selected from Aurangabad City. The Sample consisted of 800 Ss studying in 8th and 9th Std. The age range of the Ss was 13 to 15 years. The male female ratio was 1:1. At the second stage sample consisted of 400 Ss, only. It so happened, because at the second stage the nature of analysis of data was based on a 2 X 2 X 2 factorial design. In order to be included in the effective each S had to meet three criteria. At the first stage the Ss were classified in two groups (1) Joint family. (2) Nuclear family. In this process 125 Ss were deleted. Secondly, the Ss were classified on the basis of male female. In this classification 150 Ss were deleted. At the third Stage, Ss were classified on the basis of birth order i.e First born and last born. In this process 115 Ss were deleted. Lastly, to keep equal cell frequencies, 10 Ss were deleted randomly from the classified groups, where the number of Ss was more than fifty. Thus, at the second, the effective Sample of the present study consisted of 400 Ss.

Tools

Differential Personality Inventory (DPI):

This test is developed and standardized by L.N.K. Shinha and Arun Kumar Singh. The test consisted of 165 Items. The subjects were required to respond to each item in terms of 'True' OR 'False'. The test – retest Reliability Coefficient Range from .73 to .86 which were high and significant indicating that the Different dimensions of the Scale have sufficient Temporal Stability.

Neurosis Measurement Scale (NMS):

This test is developed and standardized by Dr. M.P. Uniyal and Dr. Km. Abha rani bisht. The test consisted of 70 Items and Five Alternatives. 'Always', 'Often', 'Sometimes', 'Rarely', and 'Never'. The reliability of the scale was determined by test-retest method. The retest was done after two different time intervals one month coefficient reliability .81 and 45 days coefficient reliability .79 and the scale has congruent validity with kundu's neurotic personality inventory.

136

Procedures of data collection

Each of the two instruments will be administered individuals as well as a small group. While collecting the data for the study the later approaches were adopted. The subjects were called in a small group of 20 to 25 subjects and their seating arrangements were made in a classroom. Prior to administration of test, through informal talk appropriate rapport was established. At first, differential personality scale was distributed to the Ss. they were asked to read the instructions given on the first page. After that they were asked to write the answers as fast as they can. Filled copies of scale were collected. After five minutes rest Neurosis Measurement Scale was given to the Ss. Following the same procedure whole data were collected.

Variable under study

Independent variable-

1. Types of family
2. Sex
3. Birth Order

Dependent Variable

1) Decisiveness

2) Responsibility

3) Emotional stability

4) Masculinity

5) Friendliness

6) Heterosexuality

7) Ego Strength

8) Curiosity

9) Dominance

10) Phobic Reaction

Design of Study:

In the present study joint family Vs Nuclear family, male Vs female, First Born Vs Last Born were treated is independent variables. Nine personality factor and phobic reaction were the dependent variables. Thus, a 2 x 2 x 2 balanced factorial design was used.

Statistical treatment of Data:

First the data were subjected to mean, standard deviation and correlation. Then three way analysis of variance was applied.

Discussion:

Results were discussed considering the statistical values obtained and relevant hypotheses.

Chapter – IV
Statistical Treatment

When we attempt to describe an individual's personality, we attempt to describe an individual's personality, we usually do so in terms of specific aspects of personality, called traits. A personality trait is a durable disposition to behave in a particular way in a variety of situations. Adjectives such as honest, dependable, moody, impulsive, suspicious, anxious, excitable, domineering, and friendly describe dispositions that represent personality traits.

Most trait theories of personality, such as those of Gordon Allport (1937' 1961) and Raymond Cattell (1950, 1966) assume that some traits are more basic than others. According to this notion, a small number of fundamental traits determine other, more superficial traits. For example, a person's tendency to be impulsive, restless, irritable, boisterous, and impatient might all derive from a more basic tendency to be excitable.

In recent years, Robert McCrae and Paul Costa (1987,1997,1999) have stimulated a lively debate among psychologists by arguing that the vast majority of personality traits derive from just five higher order traits that have come to be known as the "Big Five": extraversion, neuroticism, openness to experience, agreeableness, and conscientiousness.

The present study aimed at to study the strength of association between personality & phobic reaction, and find out the effect of type of family, sex, & birth order on personality of children. The Table no 4.1 shows the relationship between Personality and Phobic Reaction among Ss

Table No.4.1

r Showing the relationship between Personality and Phobic Reaction among Ss

Variable	N	DF	r	P
Decisiveness	400			
Phobic Reaction	400	798	-0.16	< .01

The results displayed in table No.01 Clearly Indicated the significant Negative Correlation between Decisiveness and Phobic Reaction (r = - 0.16, df= 798 and P > .01) means high score decisiveness Ss shows less phobic reaction.

Table No.4.2

r Showing the relationship between Personality and Phobic Reaction among Ss

Variable	N	DF	r	P
Responsibilities	400			
Phobic Reaction	400	798	-0.33	< .01

The results displayed in table No.02 Clearly Indicated the significant Negative Correlation between Responsibilities and Phobic Reaction (r = - 0.33, df= 798 and P > .01) means high score of responsibility Ss no phobic reaction.

Table No.4.3

r Showing the relationship between Personality and Phobic Reaction among Ss

Variable	N	DF	r	P
Emotional Stability	400			
Phobic Reaction	400	798	0.56	< .01

The results displayed in table No.4.3 Clearly Indicated the significant positive Correlation between Emotional Stability and Phobic Reaction (r =0.56, df=798 and P < .01) means low emotional stability scores Ss high phobic reaction.

Table No.4.4

r Showing the relationship between Personality and Phobic Reaction among Ss

Variable	N	DF	r	P
Masculinity	400			
Phobic Reaction	400	798	0.08	NS

The results displayed in table No.4.4 Clearly Indicated the significant Zero Correlation between Masculinity and Phobic Reaction (r =0.08, df=798 and NS) means no directly correlation in between masculinity and Phobic Reaction.

Table No.4.5

r Showing the relationship between Personality and Phobic Reaction among Ss

Variable	N	DF	r	P
Friendliness	400			
Phobic Reaction	400	798	-0.45	< .01

The results displayed in table No.05 Clearly Indicated the significant Negative Correlation between Friendliness and Phobic Reaction (r = -0.45, df=798 and P < .01) means high score Friendliness Ss no phobic reaction.

Table No.4.6

r Showing the relationship between Personality and Phobic Reaction among Ss

Variable	N	DF	r	P
Hetero-Sexuality	400			
Phobic Reaction	400	798	0.11	NS

The results displayed in table No.4.6 Clearly Indicated the significant Zero Correlation between Heterosexuality and Phobic Reaction (r =0.11, df=798 and NS)

Table No.4.7

r Showing the relationship between Personality and Phobic Reaction among Ss

Variable	N	DF	r	P
Ego Strength	400			
Phobic Reaction	400	798	0.72	< .01

The results displayed in table No.4.7 Clearly Indicated the significant positive Correlation between Ego Strength and Phobic Reaction (r =0.72, df=798 and P < .01) means high ego strength score Ss high phobic reaction.

Table No.4.8

r Showing the relationship between Personality and Phobic Reaction among Ss

Variable	N	DF	r	P
Curiosity	400			
Phobic Reaction	400	798	-0.64	< .01

The results displayed in table No.4.8 Clearly Indicated the significant Negative Correlation between Curiosity and Phobic Reaction (r = -0.64, df=798 and P < .01) means no correlation in between curiosity and phobic reaction.

Table No.4.9

r Showing the relationship between Personality and Phobic Reaction among Ss

Variable	N	DF	r	P
Dominance	400			
Phobic Reaction	400	798	0.18	NS

The results displayed in table No.4.9 Clearly Indicated the not significant positive Correlation between Dominance and Phobic Reaction (r =0.20, df=798 and P < .01) means high dominance score Ss less phobic reaction.

The Decisiveness was influenced by types of family, sex and birth order were examined in the study. Means and standard deviations obtained by the eight classified groups on the measure of Decisiveness are given in table 1.1. The eight classified groups were the same, which were classified on the basis of three independent variables namely by types of family, sex and birth order.

A = Types of Family   **B = Sex**   **C =Birth Order**

A1 = Joint   A2 = Nuclear   B1 = Male   B2 = Female   C1 = First Born   C2 = Last Born

Graph No. 4.1

Variable	Group	A1 B1 C1	A1 B1 C2	A1 B2 C1	A1 B2 C2	A2 B1 C1	A2 B1 C2	A2 B2 C1	A2 B2 C2
Decisiveness	Mean	36.99	35.99	32.85	27.22	35.45	33.35	28.58	26.25
	S.D.	2.59	2.61	2.45	3.44	2.60	2.70	3.40	4.00
N	50	50	50	50	50	50	50	50	50

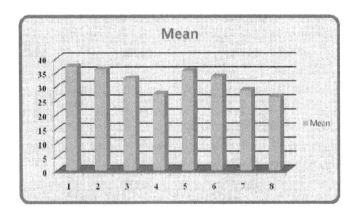

Means and standard deviation obtain by the eight classified groups are given in the table 1.1, it can also be seen in graph 1.1 Careful examination of the standard deviation associated with the means reveals that in all the eight classified groups the distribution of Decisiveness score is normal. Mean value shows that group A1B1C1 had the highest Decisiveness among the eight groups, while group A2B2C2 had the poorest Decisiveness. The subjects in the group A1B1C1 Joint family, having male and coming form first born. Other groups A2B2C2 include Nuclear Family with Female coming from Last Born. The other values are between these two groups differences in the largest and the smallest means is large, but whether the difference is significantly large or not could not be decided only on the basis of mean and standard deviation whether the results supported the hypothesis or not was found out only after treating the data by three way analysis of variances.

Table No. 4.11

Complete summary of three ways ANOVA for Decisiveness

Source of variation	Ss	df	Mss	F	P
A : Types of family	162.56	1	162.56	121.31**	P < 0.1
B : Sex	3019.5	1	3019.5	2253.36**	P < 0.1
C : Birth Order	673.4	1	673.4	502.54**	P < 0.1
A x B	95.06	1	95.06	70.94**	P < 0.1
A x C	7.56	1	7.56	5.64*	P < 0.5
B x C	42.9	1	42.9	32.01**	P < 0.1
A x B x C	24.52	1	24.52	18.3**	P < 0.1
Within : error	523.94	392	1.34		
Total	4549.44	399			

Graph No. 4.2
Main effect A

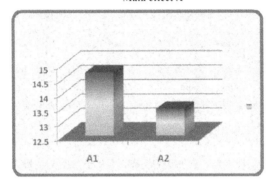

From the summary and graph no. 1.4, it is seen that main effect A is highly significant main effect A refers to the factor Types of family. It was varied at two levels i.e. Joint family and Nuclear family it was assumed Joint family and Nuclear family differ significantly with regards to Decisiveness. Since the main effect A is highly significant (F = 121.31, df = 1 and 392, P < 0.01) It is clear that Joint family and Nuclear family subjects differ significantly from each other from the mean scores and graph No. 1.4 it was found that the Joint family had significantly higher Decisiveness than the Nuclear family this results support the hypothesis.

Graph No. 4.3
Main effect B

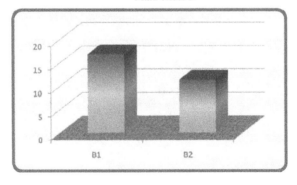

The second independent variable the factor of Sex it was also varied at two levels. The effective sample was divided in to two groups, Male and Female. Main effect B represents the factor of Sex. Main effect B has yielded highly significantly result and F value of 2253.36 for 1 and 392 df is significant beyond 0.01 level. It indicates that the subjects the Male and the subjects of Sex differ from each other significantly. If the means and Graph no. 1.5 are consider then it is seen that the mean scores Male subjects is larger than the Female subjects. It was found to Male Ss had significantly high Decisiveness than the Female Ss. This result supports the hypothesis.

Graph No. 4.4
Main effect C

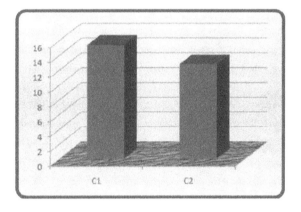

Factor of Birth Order was regarded as an important factor in the development of Decisiveness. It was assumed that subjects having first born developed significantly higher Decisiveness than the subjects having last born. To what extent the hypothesis was supported by the results was examine from the summary of ANOVA. Main effect C represent the factor of birth order, it was also varied at two level from the summary it is seen that main effect c is associated with a high F value. It's seen that in development of Decisiveness the role of birth order of most significant. An F value of 502.54, which is much larger than what is needed to be

significant at 0.01 level when df are 1 and 392, If the means and the graph no. 1.6 is consider then it is seen that the mean score of first born is larger than that of the last born subjects this results also support the hypothesis.

Though all the three main effect were highly significant result showed that, in the development of Decisiveness, this factor were not functioning independently. This could be seen from the interaction effects. Interaction A x B has brought out and F value of 70.94 which is much larger than what is needed to be significant at 0.01 level when the df are 1 and 392 in other words main effect A and main effect B are interdependent on each other.

Interaction A x C is also significant (F = 5.64, df = 1 & 392, P < 0.05) it means main effect A and C are dependent on each other.

Interaction B x C has brought out and f value of 32.01, which is much larger than what is needed to which significant at 0.01 level when the df are 1 and 392 in other works main effect B & main effect C are interdependent.

Interaction A x B x C is significant (F = 18.3, df = 1 & 392, P < 0.01), which suggest that all the three independent variables namely types of family sex, and birth order are interdependent on each other.

The Respocibility was influenced by types of family, sex and birth order were examined in the study. Means and standard deviations obtained by the eight classified groups on the measure of Respocibility are given in table 2.1. The eight classified groups were the same, which were classified on the basis of three independent variables namely by types of family, sex and birth order.

Table 4.13

Shows means and standard deviations for Responsibility

	$A_1B_1C_1$	$A_1B_1C_2$	$A_1B_2C_1$	$A_1B_2C_2$	$A_2B_1C_1$	$A_2B_1C_2$	$A_2B_2C_1$	$A_2B_2C_2$
Mean	14.84	12.5	9.84	8.34	12.96	11.04	8.72	6.4
SD	0.86	0.99	0.93	0.72	1.03	0.86	0.86	1.25
N	50	50	50	50	50	50	50	50

Graph No. 4.5

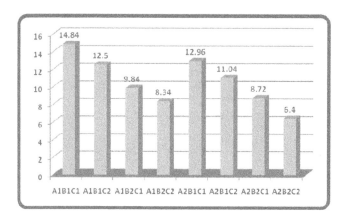

Examination of means and standard deviations of the eight classified group's show that in most of the groups scores obtained on Responsibility are more or less

148

normally distributed. On this measure, high score denotes high Responsibility, so, if the mean scores are examined then all the groups had shown more or less normal Responsibility, but among them some are relatively high Responsibility, others are not. A2B2C1 obtained a mean score of 14.84 (SD= 0.86), indicating that, the group was relatively high Responsibility among the eight groups. There were three groups which exhibited relatively low Responsibility, these groups were Gr. $A_2B_1C_1$ (Mean= 12.96, SD=1.03); Gr. $A_2B_1C_2$ (Mean = 11.04, SD= 0.86) and Gr. $A_2B_2C_2$ (Mean =6.4, SD= 1.25). Thus, the eight groups varied remarkably in Responsibility from each other. These data when treated by three way ANOVA, following results were obtained.

Table No. 4.14

Complete summary of three ways ANOVA for Responsibility

Source of variation	Ss	df	Mss	F	P
A : Types of family	256	1	256	284.44**	P < 0.1
B : Sex	2034.01	1	2034.01	2260.01**	P < 0.1
C : Birth Order	408.04	1	408.04	453.38	P < 0.1
A x B	0.49	1	0.49	0.54	NS
A x C	1	1	1	1.11	NS
B x C	1.21	1	1.21	1.34	NS
A x B x C	9.61	1	9.61	10.68**	P < 0.1
Within : error	353.08	392	0.9		
Total	3063.44	399			

Graph No. 4.6

Main effect A

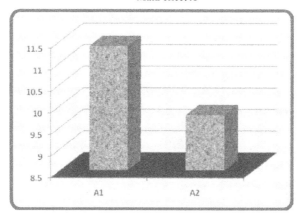

From the summary and graph no. 2.3, it is seen that main effect A is highly significant main effect A refers to the factor Types of family. It was varied at two levels i.e. Joint family and Nuclear family it was assumed Joint family and Nuclear family differ significantly with regards to Responsibility. Since the main effect A is highly significant (F = 284.44, df = 1 and 392, P < 0.01) It is clear that Joint family and Nuclear family subjects differ significantly from each other from the mean scores and graph No. 2.3 it was found that the Joint family had significantly higher Responsibility than the Nuclear family this results support the hypothesis.

Graph No. 4.7

Main effect B

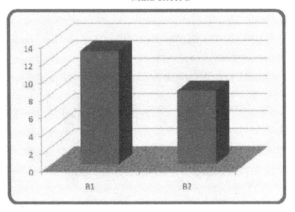

The second independent variable the factor of Sex it was also varied at two levels. The effective sample was divided in to two groups, Male and Female. Main effect B represents the factor of Sex. Main effect B has yielded highly significantly result and F value of 2260.01 for 1 and 392 df is significant beyond 0.01 level. It indicates that the subjects the Male and the subjects of Sex differ from each other significantly. If the means and Graph no. 2.4 are consider then it is seen that the mean scores Male subjects is larger than the Female subjects. It was found to Male Ss had significantly high Responsibility than the Female Ss. This result supports the hypothesis.

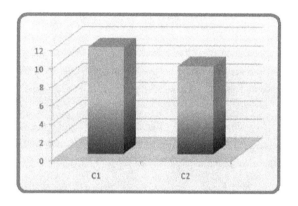

Factor of Birth Order was regarded as an important factor in the development of Responsibility. It was assumed that subjects having first born developed significantly higher Responsibility than the subjects having last born. To what extent the hypothesis was supported by the results was examine from the summary of ANOVA. Main effect C represent the factor of birth order, it was also varied at two level from the summary it is seen that main effect c is associated with a high F value. It's seen that in development of Responsibility the role of birth order of most significant. An F value of 453.38, which is much larger than what is needed to be significant at 0.01 level when df are 1 and 392, If the means and the graph no. 2.5 is consider then it is seen that the mean score of first born is larger than that of the last born subjects this results also support the hypothesis.

Though all the three main effect were highly significant result showed that, in the development of Responsibility, this factor were not functioning independently. This could be seen from the interaction effects. Interaction A x B has brought out and F value of 0.54 which is much larger than what is needed to be not significant at both level when the df are 1 and 392 in other words main effect A and main effect B are not interdependent on each other.

Interaction A x C is also significant (F = 1.11, df = 1 & 392, NS) it means main effect A and C are not dependent on each other.

Interaction B x C has brought out and f value of 1.34, which is much larger than what is needed to which not significant at both level when the df are 1 and 392 in other works main effect B & main effect C are not interdependent.

Interaction A x B x C is significant (F = 10.68, df = 1 & 392, P < 0.01), which suggest that all the three independent variables namely types of family sex, and birth order are interdependent on each other.

The Emotional Stability was influenced by types of family, sex and birth order were examined in the study. Means and standard deviations obtained by the eight classified groups on the measure of Emotional Stability are given in table 2.1. The eight classified groups were the same, which were classified on the basis of three independent variables namely by types of family, sex and birth order.

Table No. 4.15

Variable	Group	A1 B1 C1	A1 B1 C2	A1 B2 C1	A1 B2 C2	A2 B1 C1	A2 B1 C2	A2 B2 C1	A2 B2 C2
Emotional Stability	Mean	17.2	16.5	15.12	12.7	16.02	15.54	11.52	7.6
	S.D.	0.76	1.28	0.75	1.25	1.02	0.76	1.39	0.99
	N	50	50	50	50	50	50	50	50

A = Types of Family　　　　**B = Sex**　　　　**C =Birth Order**
A1 = Joint　　A2 = Nuclear　　B1 = Male　B2 = Female　C1 = First Born　C2 = Last Born

Graph No. 4.9

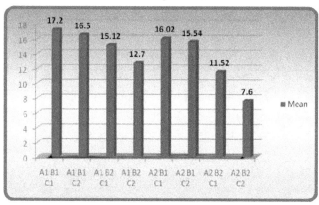

154

Means and standard deviation obtain by the eight classified groups are given in the table 3.1, it can also be seen in graph 3.2 Careful examination of the standard deviation associated with the means reveals that in all the eight classified groups the distribution of Emotional Stability score is normal. Mean value shows that group A1B1C1 had the highest Emotional Stability among the eight groups, while group A2B2C2 had the lowest Emotional Stability. The subjects in the group A1B1C1 Joint family, having male and coming form first born. Other groups A2B2C2 include Nuclear Family with Female coming from Last Born. The other values are between these two groups differences in the largest and the smallest means is large, but whether the difference is significantly large or not could not be decided only on the basis of mean and standard deviation whether the results supported the hypothesis or not was found out only after treating the data by three way analysis of variances.

Table No. 4.16

Complete summary of three ways ANOVA for Emotional Stability

Source of variation	Ss	df	Mss	F	P
A : Types of family	734.41	1	734.41	661.63**	P < 0.1
B : Sex	2097.64	1	2097.64	1889.77**	P < 0.1
C : Birth Order	353.44	1	353.44	318.41**	P < 0.1
A x B	268.96	1	268.96	242.31**	P < 0.1
A x C	10.24	1	10.24	9.23**	P < 0.1
B x C	166.41	1	166.41	149.92**	P < 0.1
A x B x C	18.49	1	18.49	16.66**	P < 0.1
Within : error	434.16	392	1.11		
Total	4083.75	399			

Main effect A

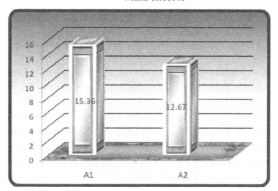

From the summary and graph no. 3.4, it is seen that main effect A is highly significant main effect A refers to the factor Types of family. It was varied at two levels i.e. Joint family and Nuclear family it was assumed Joint family and Nuclear family differ significantly with regards to Emotional Stability. Since the main effect A is highly significant (F = 661.63, df = 1 and 392, P < 0.01) It is clear that Joint family and Nuclear family subjects differ significantly from each other from the mean scores and graph No. 3.4 it was found that the Joint family had significantly higher Emotional Stability than the Nuclear family this results support the hypothesis.

Graph No. 3.5

Main effect B

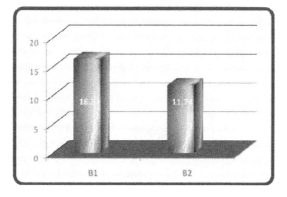

The second independent variable the factor of Sex it was also varied at two levels. The effective sample was divided in to two groups, Male and Female. Main effect B represents the factor of Sex. Main effect B has yielded highly significantly result and F value of 1889.77 for 1 and 392 df is significant beyond 0.01 level. It indicates that the subjects the Male and the subjects of Sex differ from each other significantly. If the means and Graph no. 3.5 are consider then it is seen that the mean scores Male subjects is larger than the Female subjects. It was found to Male Ss had significantly high Emotional Stability than the Female Ss. This result supports the hypothesis.

Graph No. 4.11
Main effect C

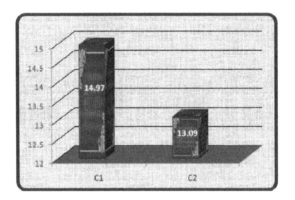

Factor of Birth Order was regarded as an important factor in the development of Emotional Stability. It was assumed that subjects having first born developed significantly higher Emotional Stability than the subjects having last born. To what extent the hypothesis was supported by the results was examine from the summary of ANOVA. Main effect C represent the factor of birth order, it was also varied at two level from the summary it is seen that main effect c is associated with a high F value. It's seen that in development of Emotional Stability the role of birth order of most significant. An F value of 318.41, which is much larger than what is needed to be

significant at 0.01 level when df are 1 and 392, If the means and the graph no. 3.6 is consider then it is seen that the mean score of first born is larger than that of the last born subjects this results also support the hypothesis.

Though all the three main effect were highly significant result showed that, in the development of Emotional Stability, this factor were not functioning independently. This could be seen from the interaction effects. Interaction A x B has brought out and F value of 242.31 which is much larger than what is needed to be significant at 0.01 level when the df are 1 and 392 in other words main effect A and main effect B are interdependent on each other.

Interaction A x C is also significant (F = 9.23, df = 1 & 392, P < 0.01) it means main effect A and C are dependent on each other.

Interaction B x C has brought out and f value of 149.92, which is much larger than what is needed to which significant at 0.01 level when the df are 1 and 392 in other works main effect B & main effect C are interdependent.

Interaction A x B x C is significant (F = 16.66, df = 1 & 392, P < 0.01), which suggest that all the three independent variables namely types of family sex, and birth order are interdependent on each other.

The Masculinity was influenced by types of family, sex and birth order were examined in the study. Means and standard deviations obtained by the eight classified groups on the measure of Masculinity are given in table 2.1. The eight classified groups were the same, which were classified on the basis of three independent variables namely by types of family, sex and birth order.

Table No. 4.18

Variable	Group	A1 B1 C1	A1 B1 C2	A1 B2 C1	A1 B2 C2	A2 B1 C1	A2 B1 C2	A2 B2 C1	A2 B2 C2
Masculinity	Mean	17.14	15.82	14.22	11.82	17.08	15.24	10.64	6.48
	S.D.	0.78	0.75	1.21	1.73	0.99	1.20	1.16	1.39
N		50	50	50	50	50	50	50	50

A = Types of Family **B = Sex** **C =Birth Order**

A1 = Joint A2 = Nuclear B1 = Male B2 = Female C1 = First Born C2 = Last Born

Graph No. 4.12

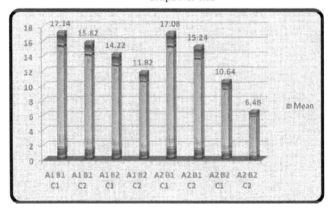

159

Means and standard deviation obtain by the eight classified groups are given in the table 4.1, it can also be seen in graph 4.1 Careful examination of the standard deviation associated with the means reveals that in all the eight classified groups the distribution of Masculinity score is normal. Mean value shows that group A1B1C1 had the highest Masculinity among the eight groups, while group A2B2C2 had the lowest Masculinity. The subjects in the group A1B1C1 Joint family, having male and coming form first born. Other groups A2B2C2 include Nuclear Family with Female coming from Last Born. The other values are between these two groups differences in the largest and the smallest means is large, but whether the difference is significantly large or not could not be decided only on the basis of mean and standard deviation whether the results supported the hypothesis or not was found out only after treating the data by three way analysis of variances.

Table No. 4.19

Complete summary of three ways ANOVA for Masculinity

Source of variation	Ss	df	Mss	F	P
A : Types of family	571.21	1	571.21	402.26**	P < 0.1
B : Sex	3058.09	1	3058.09	2153.58**	P < 0.1
C : Birth Order	590.49	1	590.49	415.84**	P < 0.1
A x B	428.49	1	428.49	301.75**	P < 0.1
A x C	32.49	1	32.49	22.88**	P < 0.1
B x C	72.25	1	72.25	50.88**	P < 0.1
A x B x C	9.61	1	9.61	6.77**	P < 0.1
Within : error	556.16	392	1.42		
Total	5318.79	399			

Main effect A

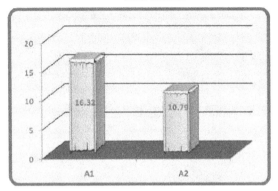

From the summary and graph no. 4.4, it is seen that main effect A is highly significant main effect A refers to the factor Types of family. It was varied at two levels i.e. Joint family and Nuclear family it was assumed Joint family and Nuclear family differ significantly with regards to Masculinity. Since the main effect A is highly significant ($F = 402.26$, $df = 1$ and 392, $P < 0.01$) It is clear that Joint family and Nuclear family subjects differ significantly from each other from the mean scores and graph No. 4.4 it was found that the Joint family had significantly higher Masculinity than the Nuclear family this results support the hypothesis.

Graph No. 4.14

Main effect B

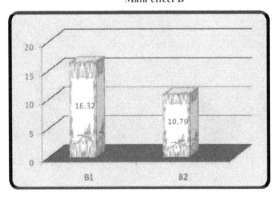

The second independent variable the factor of Sex it was also varied at two levels. The effective sample was divided in to two groups, Male and Female. Main effect B represents the factor of Sex. Main effect B has yielded highly significantly result and F value of 2153.58 for 1 and 392 df is significant beyond 0.01 level. It indicates that the subjects the Male and the subjects of Sex differ from each other significantly. If the means and Graph no. 4.5 are consider then it is seen that the mean scores Male subjects is larger than the Female subjects. It was found to Male Ss had significantly high Masculinity than the Female Ss. This result supports the hypothesis.

Graph No. 4.15
Main effect C

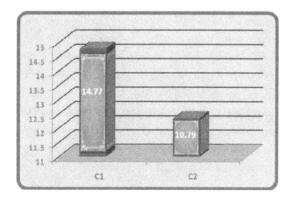

Factor of Birth Order was regarded as an important factor in the development of Masculinity. It was assumed that subjects having first born developed significantly higher Masculinity than the subjects having last born. To what extent the hypothesis was supported by the results was examine from the summary of ANOVA. Main effect C represent the factor of birth order, it was also varied at two level from the summary it is seen that main effect c is associated with a high F value. It's seen that in development of Masculinity the role of birth order of most significant. An F value of 415.84, which is much larger than what is needed to be significant at 0.01 level when df are 1 and 392, If the means and the graph no. 4.6 is consider then it is seen that the

mean score of first born is larger than that of the last born subjects this results also support the hypothesis.

Though all the three main effect were highly significant result showed that, in the development Masculinity, this factor were not functioning independently. This could be seen from the interaction effects. Interaction A x B has brought out and F value of 301.75 which is much larger than what is needed to be significant at 0.01 level when the df are 1 and 392 in other words main effect A and main effect B are interdependent on each other.

Interaction A x C is also significant (F = 22.88, df = 1 & 392, P < 0.05) it means main effect A and C are dependent on each other.

Interaction B x C has brought out and f value of 50.88, which is much larger than what is needed to which significant at 0.01 level when the df are 1 and 392 in other works main effect B & main effect C are interdependent.

Interaction A x B x C is significant (F = 6.77, df = 1 & 392, P < 0.01), which suggest that all the three independent variables namely types of family sex, and birth order are interdependent on each other.

The Friendliness was influenced by types of family, sex and birth order were examined in the study. Means and standard deviations obtained by the eight classified groups on the measure of Friendliness are given in table 5.1. The eight classified groups were the same, which were classified on the basis of three independent variables namely by types of family, sex and birth order.

Table No. 4.20

Variable	Group	A1 B1 C1	A1 B1 C2	A1 B2 C1	A1 B2 C2	A2 B1 C1	A2 B1 C2	A2 B2 C1	A2 B2 C2
Friendliness	Mean	19.04	16.58	15.44	13.14	18.06	16.6	12.38	9.58
	S.D.	1.07	1.55	1.01	1.60	1.66	1.56	1.24	1.25
N		50	50	50	50	50	50	50	50

A = Types of Family   B = Sex   C = Birth Order

A1 = Joint   A2 = Nuclear   B1 = Male   B2 = Female   C1 = First Born   C2 = Last Born

Graph No. 4.16

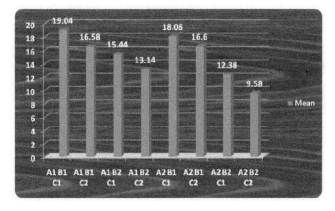

Means and standard deviation obtain by the eight classified groups are given in the table 5.1, it can also be seen in graph 5.2 Careful examination of the standard deviation associated with the means reveals that in all the eight classified groups the distribution of Friendliness score is normal. Mean value shows that group A1B1C1 had the highest Friendliness among the eight groups, while group A2B2C2 had the lowest Ego-Strength. The subjects in the group A1B1C1 Joint family, having male and coming form first born. Other groups A2B2C2 include Nuclear Family with Female coming from Last Born. The other values are between these two groups differences in the largest and the smallest means is large, but whether the difference is significantly large or not could not be decided only on the basis of mean and standard deviation whether the results supported the hypothesis or not was found out only after treating the data by three way analysis of variances.

Table No. 4.21

Complete summary of three ways ANOVA for Friendliness

Source of variation	Ss	df	Mss	F	P
A : Types of family	359.1	1	359.1	186.06**	P < 0.1
B : Sex	2435.42	1	2435.42	1261.88**	P < 0.1
C : Birth Order	508.5	1	508.5	263.47**	P < 0.1
A x B	200.22	1	200.22	103.74**	P < 0.1
A x C	1.56	1	1.56	0.81**	NS
B x C	8.7	1	8.7	4.51**	P < 0.5
A x B x C	14.08	1	14.08	7.3**	P < 0.1
Within : error	757.22	392	1.93		
Total	4284.8	399			

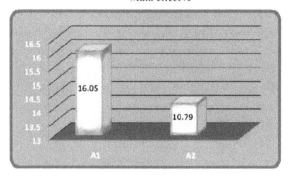

From the summary and graph no. 5.4, it is seen that main effect A is highly significant main effect A refers to the factor Types of family. It was varied at two levels i.e. Joint family and Nuclear family it was assumed Joint family and Nuclear family differ significantly with regards to Friendliness. Since the main effect A is highly significant (F = 359.1, df = 1 and 392, P < 0.01) It is clear that Joint family and Nuclear family subjects differ significantly from each other from the mean scores and graph No. 5.4 it was found that the Joint family had significantly higher Friendliness than the Nuclear family this results support the hypothesis.

Graph No. 5.5

Main effect B

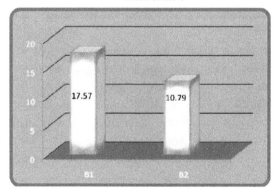

The second independent variable the factor of Sex it was also varied at two levels. The effective sample was divided in to two groups, Male and Female. Main effect B represents the factor of Sex. Main effect B has yielded highly significantly result and F value of 1261.88 for 1 and 392 df is significant beyond 0.01 level. It indicates that the subjects the Male and the subjects of Sex differ from each other significantly. If the means and Graph no. 5.5 are consider then it is seen that the mean scores Male subjects is larger than the Female subjects. It was found to Male Ss had significantly high Friendliness than the Female Ss. This result supports the hypothesis.

Graph No. 4.17

Main effect C

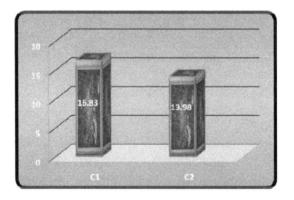

Factor of Birth Order was regarded as an important factor in the development of Friendliness. It was assumed that subjects having first born developed significantly higher Friendliness than the subjects having last born. To what extent the hypothesis was supported by the results was examine from the summary of ANOVA. Main effect C represent the factor of birth order, it was also varied at two level from the summary it is seen that main effect c is associated with a high F value. It's seen that in development of Friendliness the role of birth order of most significant. An F value of 263.47, which is much larger than what is needed to be significant at 0.01 level when df are 1 and 392, If the means and the graph no. 5.6 is consider then it is seen that the mean score of first born is larger than that of the last born subjects this results also support the hypothesis.

Though all the three main effect were highly significant result showed that, in the development Friendliness, this factor were not functioning independently. This could be seen from the interaction effects. Interaction A x B has brought out and F value of 103.74 which is much larger than what is needed to be significant at 0.01 level when the df are 1 and 392 in other words main effect A and main effect B are interdependent on each other.

Interaction A x C is also not significant ($F = 0.81$, df = 1 & 392) it means main effect A and C are not dependent on each other.

Interaction B x C has brought out and f value of 4.51, which is much larger than what is needed to which significant at 0.05 level when the df are 1 and 392 in other works main effect B & main effect C are interdependent.

Interaction A x B x C is significant ($F = 7.3$, df = 1 & 392, $P < 0.01$), which suggest that all the three independent variables namely types of family sex, and birth order are interdependent on each other.

The Heterosexuality was influenced by types of family, sex and birth order were examined in the study. Means and standard deviations obtained by the eight classified groups on the measure of Heterosexuality are given in table 6.1. The eight classified groups were the same, which were classified on the basis of three independent variables namely by types of family, sex and birth order.

Table No. 4.22

Variable	Group	A1 B1 C1	A1 B1 C2	A1 B2 C1	A1 B2 C2	A2 B1 C1	A2 B1 C2	A2 B2 C1	A2 B2 C2
Heterosexuality	Mean	18.2	16.78	15.38	10.4	16.84	15.88	11.8	8.86
	S.D.	0.81	1.40	1.55	0.90	1.63	1.38	1.40	1.42
	N	50	50	50	50	50	50	50	50

A = Types of Family   **B = Sex**   **C = Birth Order**

A1 = Joint   A2 = Nuclear   B1 = Male   B2 = Female   C1 = First Born   C2 = Last Born

Graph No. 4.18

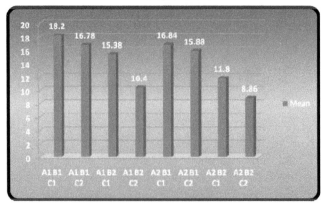

Means and standard deviation obtain by the eight classified groups are given in the table 6.1, it can also be seen in graph 6.2 Careful examination of the standard deviation associated with the means reveals that in all the eight classified groups the distribution of Heterosexuality score is normal. Mean value shows that group A1B1C1 had the highest Heterosexuality among the eight groups, while group A2B2C2 had the lowest Heterosexuality. The subjects in the group A1B1C1 Joint family, having male and coming form first born. Other groups A2B2C2 include Nuclear Family with Female coming from Last Born. The other values are between these two groups differences in the largest and the smallest means is large, but whether the difference is significantly large or not could not be decided only on the basis of mean and standard deviation whether the results supported the hypothesis or not was found out only after treating the data by three way analysis of variances.

Table No. 4.23

Complete summary of three ways ANOVA for Heterosexuality

Source of variation	Ss	df	Mss	F	P
A : Types of family	340.4	1	340.4	189.11**	$P < 0.1$
B : Sex	2824.92	1	2824.92	1569.4**	$P < 0.1$
C : Birth Order	663.06	1	663.06	368.37**	$P < 0.1$
A x B	51.12	1	51.12	28.4**	$P < 0.1$
A x C	39.06	1	39.06	21.7**	$P < 0.1$
B x C	191.82	1	191.82	106.57**	$P < 0.1$
A x B x C	15.62	1	15.62	8.68**	$P < 0.1$
Within : error	704.38	392	1.8		
Total	4830.38	399			

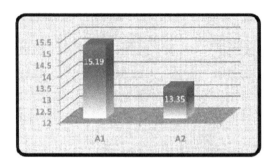

From the summary and graph no. 6.4, it is seen that main effect A is highly significant main effect A refers to the factor Types of family. It was varied at two levels i.e. Joint family and Nuclear family it was assumed Joint family and Nuclear family differ significantly with regards to Heterosexuality. Since the main effect A is highly significant (F = 189.11, df = 1 and 392, P < 0.01) It is clear that Joint family and Nuclear family subjects differ significantly from each other from the mean scores and graph No. 6.4 it was found that the Joint family had significantly higher Heterosexuality than the Nuclear family this results support the hypothesis.

Main effect B

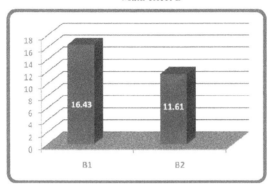

The second independent variable the factor of Sex it was also varied at two levels. The effective sample was divided in to two groups, Male and Female. Main effect B represents the factor of Sex. Main effect B has yielded highly significantly result and F value of 1569.4 for 1 and 392 df is significant beyond 0.01 level. It indicates that the subjects the Male and the subjects of Sex differ from each other significantly. If the means and Graph no. 6.5 are consider then it is seen that the mean scores Male subjects is larger than the Female subjects. It was found to Male Ss had significantly high Heterosexuality than the Female Ss. This result supports the hypothesis.

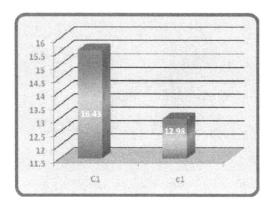

Factor of Birth Order was regarded as an important factor in the development of Heterosexuality. It was assumed that subjects having first born developed significantly higher Heterosexuality than the subjects having last born. To what extent the hypothesis was supported by the results was examine from the summary of ANOVA. Main effect C represent the factor of birth order, it was also varied at two level from the summary it is seen that main effect c is associated with a high F value. It's seen that in development of Heterosexuality the role of birth order of most significant. An F value of 368.37, which is much larger than what is needed to be significant at 0.01 level when df are 1 and 392, If the means and the graph no. 6.6 is consider then it is seen that the mean score of first born is larger than that of the last born subjects this results also support the hypothesis.

Though all the three main effect were highly significant result showed that, in the development Heterosexuality, this factor were not functioning independently. This could be seen from the interaction effects. Interaction A x B has brought out and F value of 28.4 which is much larger than what is needed to be significant at 0.01 level when the df are 1 and 392 in other words main effect A and main effect B are interdependent on each other.

Interaction A x C is also significant (F = 21.7, df = 1 & 392, P < 0.01) it means main effect A and C are dependent on each other.

Interaction B x C has brought out and f value of 106.57, which is much larger than what is needed to which significant at 0.01 level when the df are 1 and 392 in other works main effect B & main effect C are interdependent.

Interaction A x B x C is significant (F = 8.68, df = 1 & 392, P < 0.01), which suggest that all the three independent variables namely types of family sex, and birth order are interdependent on each other.

The Ego-Strength was influenced by types of family, sex and birth order were examined in the study. Means and standard deviations obtained by the eight classified groups on the measure of Ego-Strength are given in table 7.1. The eight classified groups were the same, which were classified on the basis of three independent variables namely by types of family, sex and birth order.

Table No. 7.1

Variable	Group	A1 B1 C1	A1 B1 C2	A1 B2 C1	A1 B2 C2	A2 B1 C1	A2 B1 C2	A2 B2 C1	A2 B2 C2
Ego-Strength	Mean	17.94	16.36	14.32	10.66	17.38	15.6	10.78	7.2
	S.D.	0.96	1.75	1.30	1.04	1.60	1.53	1.31	1.31
N		50	50	50	50	50	50	50	50

A = Types of Family   **B = Sex**   **C = Birth Order**

A1 = Joint   A2 = Nuclear   B1 = Male   B2 = Female   C1 = First Born   C2 = Last Born

Graph No. 4.22

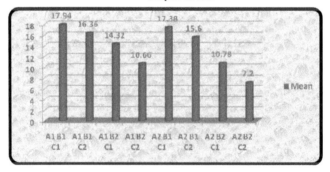

Means and standard deviation obtain by the eight classified groups are given in the table 7.1, it can also be seen in graph 7.2 Careful examination of the standard deviation associated with the means reveals that in all the eight classified groups the distribution of Ego Strength score is normal. Mean value shows that group A1B1C1 had the highest Ego Strength among the eight groups, while group A2B2C2 had the lowest Ego-Strength. The subjects in the group A1B1C1 Joint family, having male and coming form first born. Other groups A2B2C2 include Nuclear Family with Female coming from Last Born. The other values are between these two groups differences in the largest and the smallest means is large, but whether the difference is significantly large or not could not be decided only on the basis of mean and standard deviation whether the results supported the hypothesis or not was found out only after treating the data by three way analysis of variances.

Table No. 4.25

Complete summary of three ways ANOVA for Ego-Strength

Source of variation	Ss	df	Mss	F	P
A : Types of family	432.64	1	432.64	230.13**	P < 0.1
B : Sex	3696.64	1	3696.64	1966.3**	P < 0.1
C : Birth Order	702.64	1	702.64	373.54**	P < 0.1
A x B	201.64	1	201.64	107.26**	P < 0.1
A x C	0.09	1	0.09	0.05	NS
B x C	94.09	1	94.09	50.05**	P < 0.1
A x B x C	0.49	1	0.49	0.26	NS
Within : error	738.8	392	1.88		
Total	5866.64	399			

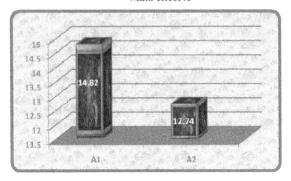

From the summary and graph no. 7.4, it is seen that main effect A is highly significant main effect A refers to the factor Types of family. It was varied at two levels i.e. Joint family and Nuclear family it was assumed Joint family and Nuclear family differ significantly with regards to Ego Strength. Since the main effect A is highly significant (F = 230.13, df = 1 and 392, P < 0.01) It is clear that Joint family and Nuclear family subjects differ significantly from each other from the mean scores and graph No. 7.4 it was found that the Joint family had significantly higher Ego Strength than the Nuclear family this results support the hypothesis.

Graph No. 4.24

Main effect B

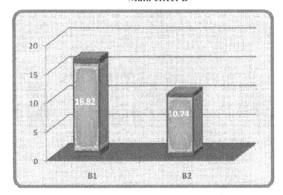

The second independent variable the factor of Sex it was also varied at two levels. The effective sample was divided in to two groups, Male and Female. Main effect B represents the factor of Sex. Main effect B has yielded highly significantly result and F value of 1966.3 for 1 and 392 df is significant beyond 0.01 level. It indicates that the subjects the Male and the subjects of Sex differ from each other significantly. If the means and Graph no. 7.5 are consider then it is seen that the mean scores Male subjects is larger than the Female subjects. It was found to Male Ss had significantly high Ego Strength than the Female Ss. This result supports the hypothesis.

Graph No. 4.25
Main effect C

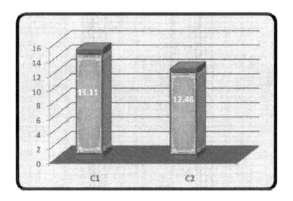

Factor of Birth Order was regarded as an important factor in the development of Ego Strength. It was assumed that subjects having first born developed significantly higher Ego Strength than the subjects having last born. To what extent the hypothesis was supported by the results was examine from the summary of ANOVA. Main effect C represent the factor of birth order, it was also varied at two level from the summary it is seen that main effect c is associated with a high F value. It's seen that in development of Ego Strength the role of birth order of most significant. An F value of 373.54, which is much larger than what is needed to be

significant at 0.01 level when df are 1 and 392, If the means and the graph no. 7.6 is consider then it is seen that the mean score of first born is larger than that of the last born subjects this results also support the hypothesis.

Though all the three main effect were highly significant result showed that, in the development Ego Strength, this factor were not functioning independently. This could be seen from the interaction effects. Interaction A x B has brought out and F value of 107.26 which is much larger than what is needed to be significant at 0.01 level when the df are 1 and 392 in other words main effect A and main effect B are interdependent on each other.

Interaction A x C is also not significant (F = 0.05, df = 1 & 392) it means main effect A and C are not dependent on each other.

Interaction B x C has brought out and f value of 50.05, which is much larger than what is needed to which significant at 0.01 level when the df are 1 and 392 in other works main effect B & main effect C are interdependent.

Interaction A x B x C is significant (F = 0.26, df = 1 & 392), which suggest that all the three independent variables namely types of family sex, and birth order are not interdependent on each other.

The Curiosity was influenced by types of family, sex and birth order were examined in the study. Means and standard deviations obtained by the eight classified groups on the measure of Curiosity are given in table 8.1. The eight classified groups were the same, which were classified on the basis of three independent variables namely by types of family, sex and birth order.

Table No. 4.26

Variable	Group	A1 B1 C1	A1 B1 C2	A1 B2 C1	A1 B2 C2	A2 B1 C1	A2 B1 C2	A2 B2 C1	A2 B2 C2
Curiosity	Mean	17.26	15.42	12.04	9.66	16.48	15.58	12.36	6.68
	S.D.	0.83	1.03	1.28	1.19	1.34	1.25	1.50	1.39
	N	50	50	50	50	50	50	50	50

A = Types of Family   **B = Sex**   **C =Birth Order**

A1 = Joint   A2 = Nuclear   B1 = Male   B2 = Female   C1 = First Born   C2 = Last Born

Graph No. 4.26

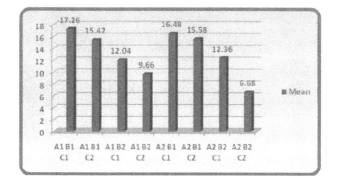

Means and standard deviation obtain by the eight classified groups are given in the table 8.1, it can also be seen in graph 8.2 Careful examination of the standard deviation associated with the means reveals that in all the eight classified groups the distribution of Curiosity score is normal. Mean value shows that group A1B1C1 had the highest Curiosity among the eight groups, while group A2B2C2 had the lowest Curiosity. The subjects in the group A1B1C1 Joint family, having male and coming form first born. Other groups A2B2C2 include Nuclear Family with Female coming from Last Born. The other values are between these two groups differences in the largest and the smallest means is large, but whether the difference is significantly large or not could not be decided only on the basis of mean and standard deviation whether the results supported the hypothesis or not was found out only after treating the data by three way analysis of variances.

Table No. 4.27

Complete summary of three ways ANOVA for Curiosity

Source of variation	Ss	df	Mss	F	P
A : Types of family	67.24	1	67.24	43.66**	P < 0.1
B : Sex	3600	1	3600	2337.66**	P < 0.1
C : Birth Order	729	1	729	473.38**	P < 0.1
A x B	26.01	1	26.01	16.89**	P < 0.1
A x C	34.81	1	34.81	22.6**	P < 0.1
B x C	176.89	1	176.89	114.86**	P < 0.1
A x B x C	112.36	1	112.36	72.86**	P < 0.1
Within : error	604	392	1.54		
Total	5350.31	399			

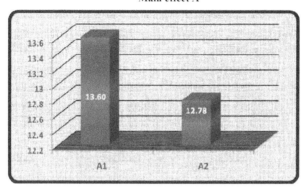

From the summary and graph no. 8.4, it is seen that main effect A is highly significant main effect A refers to the factor Types of family. It was varied at two levels i.e. Joint family and Nuclear family it was assumed Joint family and Nuclear family differ significantly with regards to Curiosity. Since the main effect A is highly significant (F = 43.66, df = 1 and 392, P < 0.01) It is clear that Joint family and Nuclear family subjects differ significantly from each other from the mean scores and graph No.8.4 it was found that the Joint family had significantly higher Curiosity than the Nuclear family this results support the hypothesis.

Graph No. 4.28

Main effect B

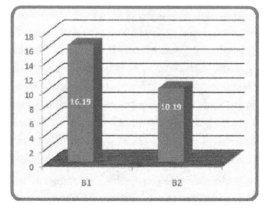

The second independent variable the factor of Sex it was also varied at two levels. The effective sample was divided in to two groups, Male and Female. Main effect B represents the factor of Sex. Main effect B has yielded highly significantly result and F value of 2337.66 for 1 and 392 df is significant beyond 0.01 level. It indicates that the subjects the Male and the subjects of Sex differ from each other significantly. If the means and Graph no. 1.5 are consider then it is seen that the mean scores Male subjects is larger than the Female subjects. It was found to Male Ss had significantly high Curiosity than the Female Ss. This result supports the hypothesis.

Graph No. 4.29

Main effect C

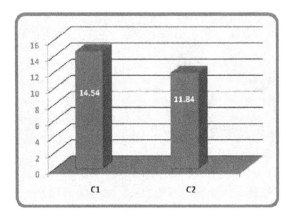

Factor of Birth Order was regarded as an important factor in the development of Curiosity. It was assumed that subjects having first born developed significantly higher Curiosity than the subjects having last born. To what extent the hypothesis was supported by the results was examine from the summary of ANOVA. Main effect C represent the factor of birth order, it was also varied at two level from the summary it is seen that main effect c is associated with a high F value. It's seen that in development of Curiosity the role of birth order of most significant. An F value of 473.38, which is much larger than what is needed to be significant at 0.01 level when df are 1 and 392, If the means and the graph no. 8.6 is consider then it is seen that the

mean score of first born is larger than that of the last born subjects this results also support the hypothesis.

Though all the three main effect were highly significant result showed that, in the development Curiosity, this factor were not functioning independently. This could be seen from the interaction effects. Interaction A x B has brought out and F value of 16.89 which is much larger than what is needed to be significant at 0.01 level when the df are 1 and 392 in other words main effect A and main effect B are interdependent on each other.

Interaction A x C is also significant (F = 22.6, df = 1 & 392, P < 0.05) it means main effect A and C are dependent on each other.

Interaction B x C has brought out and f value of 114.86, which is much larger than what is needed to which significant at 0.01 level when the df are 1 and 392 in other works main effect B & main effect C are interdependent.

Interaction A x B x C is significant (F = 72.86, df = 1 & 392, P < 0.01), which suggest that all the three independent variables namely types of family sex, and birth order are interdependent on each other.

The Dominance was influenced by types of family, sex and birth order were examined in the study. Means and standard deviations obtained by the eight classified groups on the measure of Dominance are given in table 9.1. The eight classified groups were the same, which were classified on the basis of three independent variables namely by types of family, sex and birth order.

Table No. 4.28

Variable	Group	A1 B1 C1	A1 B1 C2	A1 B2 C1	A1 B2 C2	A2 B1 C1	A2 B1 C2	A2 B2 C1	A2 B2 C2
Dominance	Mean	16.12	14.78	11.42	9.16	15.32	13.96	10.1	6.94
	S.D.	0.85	1.17	0.95	1.11	1.53	1.40	1.42	1.72
N		50	50	50	50	50	50	50	50

A = Types of Family   B = Sex   C =Birth Order

A1 = Joint   A2 = Nuclear   B1 = Male   B2 = Female   C1 = First Born   C2 = Last Born

Graph No. 4.30

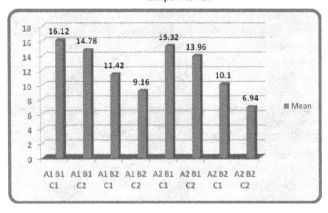

185

Means and standard deviation obtain by the eight classified groups are given in the table 9.1, it can also be seen in graph 9.2 Careful examination of the standard deviation associated with the means reveals that in all the eight classified groups the distribution of Dominance score is normal. Mean value shows that group A1B1C1 had the highest Dominance among the eight groups, while group A2B2C2 had the lowest Ego-Strength. The subjects in the group A1B1C1 Joint family, having male and coming form first born. Other groups A2B2C2 include Nuclear Family with Female coming from Last Born. The other values are between these two groups differences in the largest and the smallest means is large, but whether the difference is significantly large or not could not be decided only on the basis of mean and standard deviation whether the results supported the hypothesis or not was found out only after treating the data by three way analysis of variances.

Table No. 4.29

Complete summary of three ways ANOVA for Dominance

Source of variation	Ss	df	Mss	F	P
A : Types of family	166.41	1	166.41	98.47**	P < 0.1
B : Sex	3180.96	1	3180.96	1882.22**	P < 0.1
C : Birth Order	412.09	1	412.09	243.84**	P < 0.1
A x B	23.04	1	23.04	13.63**	P < 0.1
A x C	5.29	1	5.29	3.13	NS
B x C	46.24	1	46.24	27.36**	P < 0.1
A x B x C	4.84	1	4.84	2.86	NS
Within : error	660.88	392	1.69		
Total	4499.75	399			

Graph No. 4.31

Main effect A

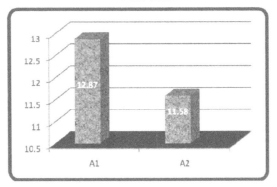

From the summary and graph no. 1.4, it is seen that main effect A is highly significant main effect A refers to the factor Types of family. It was varied at two levels i.e. Joint family and Nuclear family it was assumed Joint family and Nuclear family differ significantly with regards to Dominance. Since the main effect A is highly significant (F = 98.47, df = 1 and 392, P < 0.01) It is clear that Joint family and Nuclear family subjects differ significantly from each other from the mean scores and graph No. 3.4 it was found that the Joint family had significantly higher Dominance than the Nuclear family this results support the hypothesis.

Graph No. 9.5

Main effect B

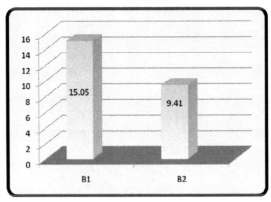

The second independent variable the factor of Sex it was also varied at two levels. The effective sample was divided in to two groups, Male and Female. Main effect B represents the factor of Sex. Main effect B has yielded highly significantly result and F value of 1882.22 for 1 and 392 df is significant beyond 0.01 level. It indicates that the subjects the Male and the subjects of Sex differ from each other significantly. If the means and Graph no. 9.5 are consider then it is seen that the mean scores Male subjects is larger than the Female subjects. It was found to Male Ss had significantly high Dominance than the Female Ss. This result supports the hypothesis.

Graph No. 4.32

Main effect C

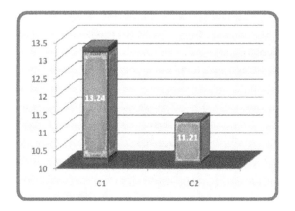

Factor of Birth Order was regarded as an important factor in the development of Dominance. It was assumed that subjects having first born developed significantly higher Dominance than the subjects having last born. To what extent the hypothesis was supported by the results was examine from the summary of ANOVA. Main effect C represent the factor of birth order, it was also varied at two level from the summary it is seen that main effect c is associated with a high F value. It's seen that in development of Dominance the role of birth order of most significant. An F value of 243.84, which is much larger than what is needed to be significant at 0.01 level when df are 1 and 392, If the means and the graph no. 9.6 is consider then it is seen that the

mean score of first born is larger than that of the last born subjects this results also support the hypothesis.

Though all the three main effect were highly significant result showed that, in the development Dominance, this factor were not functioning independently. This could be seen from the interaction effects. Interaction A x B has brought out and F value of 13.63 which is much larger than what is needed to be significant at 0.01 level when the df are 1 and 392 in other words main effect A and main effect B are interdependent on each other.

Interaction A x C is also significant (F = 3.13, df = 1 & 392) it means main effect A and C are not dependent on each other.

Interaction B x C has brought out and f value of 29.36, which is much larger than what is needed to which significant at 0.01 level when the df are 1 and 392 in other works main effect B & main effect C are interdependent.

Interaction A x B x C is not significant (F = 2.86, df = 1 & 392), which suggest that all the three independent variables namely types of family sex, and birth order are not interdependent on each other.

The Phobic Reaction was influenced by types of family, sex and birth order were examined in the study. Means and standard deviations obtained by the eight classified groups on the measure of Phobic Reaction are given in table 10.1. The eight classified groups were the same, which were classified on the basis of three independent variables namely by types of family, sex and birth order.

Table No. 4.30

Variable	Group	A1 B1 C1	A1 B1 C2	A1 B2 C1	A1 B2 C2	A2 B1 C1	A2 B1 C2	A2 B2 C1	A2 B2 C2
Phobic Reaction	Mean	27.54	22.6	19.2	16.54	24.88	22.4	19.12	16.28
	S.D.	1.47	1.12	0.90	1.37	1.04	1.16	1.12	1.55
N		50	50	50	50	50	50	50	50

A = Types of Family   B = Sex   C =Birth Order

A1 = Joint   A2 = Nuclear   B1 = Male   B2 = Female   C1 = First Born   C2 = Last Born

Graph No. 4.33

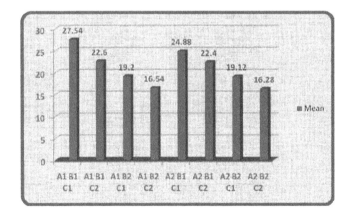

Means and standard deviation obtain by the eight classified groups are given in the table 4.1, it can also be seen in graph 4.1 Careful examination of the standard deviation associated with the means reveals that in all the eight classified groups the distribution of Phobic Reaction score is normal. Mean value shows that group A1B1C1 had the highest Phobic Reaction among the eight groups, while group A2B2C2 had the lowest Ego-Strength. The subjects in the group A1B1C1 Joint family, having male and coming form first born. Other groups A2B2C2 include Nuclear Family with Female coming from Last Born. The other values are between these two groups differences in the largest and the smallest means is large, but whether the difference is significantly large or not could not be decided only on the basis of mean and standard deviation whether the results supported the hypothesis or not was found out only after treating the data by three way analysis of variances.

Table No. 4.31

Complete summary of three ways ANOVA for Phobic Reaction

Source of variation	Ss	df	Mss	F	P
A : Types of family	64	1	64	41.83**	P < 0.1
B : Sex	4316.49	1	4316.49	2821.24**	P < 0.1
C : Birth Order	1043.29	1	1043.29	681.69**	P < 0.1
A x B	39.69	1	39.69	25.94**	P < 0.1
A x C	32.69	1	32.69	21.24**	P < 0.1
B x C	23.04	1	23.04	15.06**	P < 0.1
A x B x C	43.56	1	43.56	28.47**	P < 0.1
Within : error	599.48	392	1.53		
Total	6162.04	399			

Graph No. 4.34

Main effect A

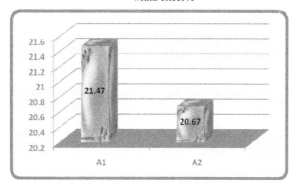

From the summary and graph no. 10.4, it is seen that main effect A is highly significant main effect A refers to the factor Types of family. It was varied at two levels i.e. Joint family and Nuclear family it was assumed Joint family and Nuclear family differ significantly with regards to Phobic Reaction. Since the main effect A is highly significant (F = 41.83, df = 1 and 392, P < 0.01) It is clear that Joint family and Nuclear family subjects differ significantly from each other from the mean scores and graph No. 10.4 it was found that the Joint family had significantly higher Phobic Reaction than the Nuclear family this results support the hypothesis.

Graph No. 4.35

Main effect B

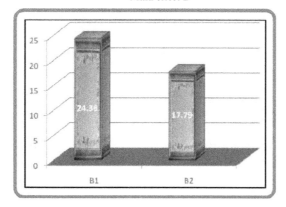

The second independent variable the factor of Sex it was also varied at two levels. The effective sample was divided in to two groups, Male and Female. Main effect B represents the factor of Sex. Main effect B has yielded highly significantly result and F value of 2821.24 for 1 and 392 df is significant beyond 0.01 level. It indicates that the subjects the Male and the subjects of Sex differ from each other significantly. If the means and Graph no. 1.5 are consider then it is seen that the mean scores Male subjects is larger than the Female subjects. It was found to Male Ss had significantly high Phobic Reaction than the Female Ss. This result supports the hypothesis.

Graph No. 4.36
Main effect C

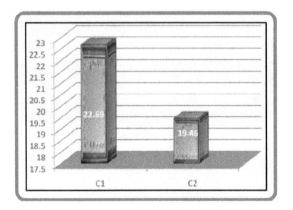

Factor of Birth Order was regarded as an important factor in the development of Phobic Reaction. It was assumed that subjects having first born developed significantly higher Phobic Reaction than the subjects having last born. To what extent the hypothesis was supported by the results was examine from the summary of ANOVA. Main effect C represent the factor of birth order, it was also varied at two level from the summary it is seen that main effect c is associated with a high F value. It's seen that in development of Phobic Reaction the role of birth order of most significant. An F value of 681.69, which is much larger than what is needed to be

significant at 0.01 level when df are 1 and 392, If the means and the graph no. 10.6 is consider then it is seen that the mean score of first born is larger than that of the last born subjects this results also support the hypothesis.

Though all the three main effect were highly significant result showed that, in the development Phobic Reaction, this factor were not functioning independently. This could be seen from the interaction effects. Interaction A x B has brought out and F value of 25.94 which is much larger than what is needed to be significant at 0.01 level when the df are 1 and 392 in other words main effect A and main effect B are interdependent on each other.

Interaction A x C is also significant (F = 21.24, df = 1 & 392, P < 0.05) it means main effect A and C are dependent on each other.

Interaction B x C has brought out and f value of 15.06, which is much larger than what is needed to which significant at 0.01 level when the df are 1 and 392 in other works main effect B & main effect C are interdependent.

Interaction A x B x C is significant (F = 28.47, df = 1 & 392, P < 0.01), which suggest that all the three independent variables namely types of family sex, and birth order are interdependent on each other.

Chapter V

DICUSSION

The causation of any particular behavior pattern is tremendously complex, and even with the information we do have it is all but impossible to predict how given circumstances will affect given individuals.

Although we may assume that the same psychological principles underlie both normal and abnormal behavior, the problem till remains of delineating the specific conditions responsible for different outcomes.

In comparison with the variables associated with biological causes of maladaptive behavior, those associated with psychosocial causes are less understood and more elusive. However a good deal has been learned about psychological and interpersonal factors that appear to play significant roles in maladaptive behavior; (a) maternal deprivation, (b) pathogenic family patterns, (c) early psychic trauma, (d) disordered interpersonal relationships, and (e) key stresses of modern life.

Again we shall see that these factors are by no means independent of each other and that a given condition may function as a primary, predisposing, precipitating, or reinforcing cause.

Maternal deprivation

Faulty development has been observed in infants deprived of maternal stimulation (or "mothering") as a consequence of either (a) separation from the mother and placement in an institution, lack of adequate "mothering" in the home. Although the emphasis here is on maternal deprivation, we are essentially concerned with warmth and stimulation, whether it be supplied by the mother, father, or other persons responsible for the child's rearing.

The effects of maternal deprivation vary considerably from infant to infant, and babies in other societies appear to thrive under widely differing conditions of maternal care. Also, the effects of unfavorable conditions during the first year of life are not always as irreversible as many investigators have thought. For example, Kagan (1973) found that Guatemalan Indian infants raised during their first year in a psychologically impoverished environment - due to the custom of the culture - were severely retarded in their development, as compared with American raised infants. However, after the first year, the environment of these infants was enriched, and by the age of 11, they performed as well or better than American children on problem-solving and related intellectual tasks.

Despite such encouraging findings, available evidence leaves little doubt that severe and sustained maternal deprivation- whether it involves growing up in an institution with restricted stimulation or suffering masked deprivation in the home - can seriously retard intellectual, emotional, social, and even physical development. The actual nature and extent of the damage resulting from maternal deprivation appear to depend on: (a) the age at which deprivation first occurs; (b) the extent and duration of such deprivation; (c) the constitutional makeup of the infant; and (d) the substitute care, if any that is provided. For example, mother surrogates or nursery schools may provide needed stimulation and loving care, thus preventing harmful effects to the infants of working mothers. However, in cases of early and prolonged deprivation, the damage to the infant may be irreversible or only partially reversible despite later corrective experiences.

Pathogenic family patterns

As the infant progresses into childhood, he must master few competencies, learn usable assumptions about him self and the world, and exert increasing inner control over his behavior.

During this period, the family unit remains the crucial guiding influence in the child's parental separation or loss as a traumatic experience personality development; unfortunately, faulty family patterns are a fertile source of unhealthy development and maladjustment. In fact, the Joint Commission on Mental Health of Children (1970) estimated that the parents of one-fourth of the nation's children are inadequate.

In view of the incidence of pathogenic family patterns, we shall deal with this problem in some detail. It may be emphasized, however, that parent-child relationships and family interactions are extremely complex matters. Thus caution is considered essential in applying given patterns to the explanation of specific cases of maladaptive behavior.

Faulty parent-child relationships

Several types of specific parent-child patterns appear with great regularity in the background of children who show emotional disturbances and other types of faulty development. Seven of these patterns will be discussed here.

1. **Rejection :** Parental rejection of the child is closely related to "masked deprivation" and may be shown in various ways- by physical neglect, denial of love and affection, lack of interest in the child's activities and achievements, harsh or inconsistent punishment, failure to spend time with the child, and lack of respect for the child's rights and feelings as a person. In a minority of cases, it also involves cruel and abusive treatment. Parental rejection may be partial or complete, passive or active, and subtly or overtly cruel.

A consideration of why parents reject their children would take us too far afield, but it would appear that a large proportion of such parents have themselves been the victims of parental rejection. In this sense, lack of love has been referred to as a "communicable disease." And, of course, rejection is not a one way street; the child may be un-accepting of his parents whether or not they reject him. This pattern sometimes occurs when the parents belong to a low-status minority group of which the child is ashamed. Although the results of such rejection have not been studied systematically, it would appear that children who reject their parents deny themselves needed trials for healthy development.

2. **Overprotection and restrictiveness :** Maternal overprotection, or "momism," involves the "smothering" of the child's growth. Overprotecting mothers may watch over their children constantly, protect them from the slightest risk, overly clothe and medicate them, and make up their mind for them at every opportunity. In the case of mother-son relationships, there is often excessive physical contact, in which the mother may sloop with the child for years and be subtly seductive in her relationships with him.

Different parental motivations may lead to overprotection. An early study by Levy (1945) found that in an experimental group of abnormally protective mothers, 75 percent had little in common with their husbands. Such maternal reactions appeared to represent a compensatory type of behavior in which the mother

197

attempted, through her contact with the child, to gain satisfactions that normally should have been obtained in her marriage. It is not uncommon in such cases for the mother to call the child her "lover" and actually to encourage the child in behaviors somewhat typical of courting.

3. **Over permissiveness and indulgence :** Although it happens less commonly than is popularly supposed, sometimes one or both parents cater to the child's slightest whims and in so doing fail to teach and reward desirable standards of behavior. In essence, the parent surrenders the running of the hoe to an uninhibited son or daughter.

Overly indulged children are characteristically spoiled selfish, inconsiderate, and demanding. Sears (1961) found that high permissiveness and low punishment in the home were correlated positively with antisocial, aggressive behavior, particularly during middle and later childhood, Unlike rejected, emotionally deprived children, who often find it difficult to enter into warm interpersonal relationships, indulged children enter readily into such relationships but exploit people for their own purposes in the same way that they have learned to exploit their parents. In dealing with authority, such children are usually rebellious since, for so long, they have had their own way. Overly indulged children also tend to be impatient, to approach problems in an aggressive and demanding manner, and to find it difficult to accept present frustrations in the interests of long-range goals.

The fact that their important and pampered status in the home does not transfer automatically to the outside world may come as a great shock to indulged youngsters; confusion and adjustive difficulties may occur when "reality" forces them to reassess their assumptions about themselves and the world.

4. **Unrealistic demands :** Some parents place excessive pressure on their children to live up to unrealistically "high" standards. Thus they may be expected to excel in school and other activities. Where the child has the capacity for exceptionally high-level performance, things may work out; but even here the child may be under such sustained pressure that little room is left for spontaneity or development as an independent person.

Typically, however, the child is never able to quite live up to parental expectations and demands. If he improves his grad from a C to a B, he may be asked why he did not get an A. If he succeeds in getting an A, the next step is to attain the highest A in his class. The parents seem to be telling the child that he could do better if he tried, and that he is not good enough the way he is. But no matter how hard he tries, he seems to fail in the eyes of his parents and, ultimately, in his own eyes as well-a fact that results in painful frustration and self-devaluation. And in promoting failure by their excessive demands, parents also tend to discourage further effort on th child's part. Almost invariably he eventually comes to feel, " I can't do it, so why try?"

Not infrequently unrealistic parental demands focus around moral standards-particularly with regard to sex, alcohol, and related matters. Thus the parents may instill in the child the view that masturbation or any other sexual activity is terribly sinful and can lead only to moral and physical degeneration. The child who accepts such rigid parental standards is likely to develop a rigid and restricted personality and to face many guilt-arousing and self-devaluating conflicts.

5.   Faulty discipline : Parents have been particularly confused during recent years about appropriate forms of discipline. Some times a misinterpretation of psychological findings and theories has led to the view that all punishment and frustration should be avoided lest the child be "fixated" in his development. In other cases parents have resorted to excessively harsh discipline, convinced that if they "spare the rod" they will spoil the child. And in still other cases, the parents have seemed to lack general guidelines, punishing children one day and ignoring or even rewarding them the next for doing the same or similar things.

Similarly inconsistent discipline makes is difficult for the child to establish stable values for guiding his behavior. When the child is punished one time and ignored or rewarded the next for the same behavior, he is at a loss to know what behavior is appropriate. Deur and parke (1970) found that children with a history of inconsistent reward and punishment for aggressive behavior were more resistant to punishment and to the extinction of their aggressive behavior than were children who had experienced more consistent discipline. The preceding study supports earlier findings showing a high correlation between inconsistent discipline and later delinquent and criminal behavior.

6.   **Communication failure:** Parents can discourage a child from asking questions and in other ways fail to foster the "information exchange" essential for healthy personality development, for example, helping the child develop a realistic frame of reference and essential competencies. Such limited and inadequate communication patterns have commonly been attributed to socially disadvantaged families, but these patterns are by no means restricted to any one socioeconomic level.

Such patterns may take a number of forms. Some parents are too busy with their own concerns to listen to their children and try to understand the conflicts and pressures they are facing. As a consequence, these parents of ten fail to give needed support and assistance during crisis periods. Other parents may have forgotten that the world often looks different to a child or adolescent and that rapid social change can lead to a very real communication gap between generations.

7.   **Undesirable parental models :** Since children tend to observe and imitate the behavior of their parents, it is apparent that parental behavior can have a highly beneficial or detrimental effect on they way a youngster learns to perceive think, feel and act. We may consider parents as undesirable models if they have faulty reality, possibility, and value assumptions, or if they depend excessively on defense mechanisms in coping with their problems as when they consistently project the blame for their own mistakes on others, if they lie and cheat, if they refuse to face and deal realistically with family problems, or if there is a marked discrepancy between their proclaimed values and those reflected in actual behavior.

A parent who is emotionally disturbed, addicted to alcohol or drugs, or drugs, or otherwise maladjusted may also serve as an undesirable model.

There are certain other common sources of stress in our society which appear directly relevant to understanding maladaptive behavior.

Devaluating frustrations :   In contemporary life there are a number of frustrations that lead to self-devaluation and hence are particularly difficult to cope with. Among these are failure, losses, personal limitations and lack of resources, guilt, and loneliness.

1.   Failure :   The highly competitive setting   in which we live almost inevitably leads to occasional failures. No team is likely to win all the time, nor can all succeed who aspire to become movie or television stars or to achieve high political office. For each person who succeeds, there is an inevitable crop of failures. Furthermore, some people seem to court failure by setting unrealistically high goals or by undertaking new ventures without adequate preparation.

2.   Losses: Closely related to failure are the many losses that people inevitably experience-losses that people inevitably experience-losses involving objects or resources they value or individuals with whom they strongly identify.

Among the most distressing material losses are those of money and status. In our society money gives its owner security, self-esteem, and the use of desired goods and services; thus an appreciable financial loss is apt to lead to severe self-recrimination and discouragement. Similarly, loss of social status whether it stems from loss of economic position or some other cause- tends to devalue and individual in his own eyes as well as in the eyes of others.

3.   Personal limitations and lack of resources : Being "on the low end of the totem pole" with regard to material advantages and possessions is a powerful source of frustration, one afflicting members of disadvantages and possessions is a powerful source of frustration, one afflicting members of disadvantaged minorities in our society with special severity. Constantly being exposed to TV commercials and other advertising depicting desirable objects and experiences in our allegedly affluent society- while seeming to be "on the outside looking in"- can be highly frustrating for those whose aspirations and hopes seem to have been bypassed by society But probably from time to time most of us make envious status comparisons in which we see others as more favorably endowed with personal and material resources than we are.

In addition, physical handicaps and other personal limitations that restrict one's activities and possibly attractiveness to members of the opposite sex- can be highly stressful. Here again, dwelling on comparisons with others who seem more favorably endowed can unnecessarily increase frustration and self-devaluation.

4.   Guilt: To understand feelings of guilt it is useful to note that (a) various value assumptions concerning right and wrong are learned and accepted; (b) these value assumptions are than applied to the appraisal of one's own behavior; and (c) it is learned, often by hard experience, that wrongdoing leads to punishment. Thus behaving in ways that one considers immoral leads to both self-devaluation and apprehension. Because of this orientation, depressed persons commonly search back through past event, locating and exaggerating misdeeds that have presumably led to present difficulties.

Guilt is likely to be particularly stressful if it seems that nothing can be done to rectify one's misdeed. In fact, Gelven (1973) concluded that "Of all the forms of mental suffering perhaps none is as pervasive or as intense as the ache of guilt" (p.69). Since guilt is heavily infused with self-recrimination and anxiety, this conclusion seems to be well supported.

5.   Loneliness : Probably most people experience painful feelings of isolation and loneliness at some time in their lives.

Being unloved and lonely has been called "the greatest poverty." Perhaps for more people than we ever realize, the world is a lonely place.

Here it is useful to make a distinction between pathological and existential loneliness, although it is difficult to draw a line between the two. The former involves the individual who is uncommitted, unconcerned, and unloving and who does not attempt to deal with loneliness through close interpersonal relationships or commitment to the human enterprise, while the latter involves the caring, committed, loving person whose loneliness is the result of conditions beyond his or her control.

Value conflicts:

Here we shall briefly mention some core conflicts of modern life that frequently lead to such tension and inner turmoil that the individual's adjustive capacities are seriously impaired

1.   Conformity Vs nonconformity: Group pressures toward conformity inevitably Group pressures toward conformity inevitably develop as a group tries to maintain itself and achieve its goals, although the degree of conformity required varies greatly from one situation to another and from one group to another. For example, the conformity needed in a military group is considerably greater than that needed in a classroom. Even in the latter case, however, certain ground rules are established and members are under some pressure to conform to them.

Usually people are most likely to conform to the demands of groups in which they value membership and which have the greatest power to meet or to frustrate their needs. Thus it is often easier for teen-agers to repudiate adult norms than it is for them to go against peer group pressures. But adults too are likely to find it difficult to go against the expectations, demands, and pressures of peer groups that are important to them.

Thus a problem which often proves deeply disturbing is when to conform or not to conform to group expectations and pressures. Usually blind conformity or nonconformity is considered maladaptive because it represents an abdication of responsible self-direction and of ten results in behavior at odds with the individual's own values. A choice based on rational thought and decision appears most likely to serve the long-term interests of both the individual and the group.

2.   Caring Vs noninvolvement : Because of the impersonality and anonymity of modern urban society, many people find it difficult to experience a sense of relatedness to others or of concern for the human enterprise. And since efforts on behalf of others can jeopardize one's own safety, the risks associated with "getting involved" may seem too great a price to pay for helping "strangers." As Seaman (1966) has put it:

3.   Avoiding Vs facing reality: Perhaps the first requisite of maturity is the ability to see oneself and the surrounding world objectively and to make the best of realities. But this is no simple task. Reality is often unpleasant and anxiety-arousing and may undermine an individual's efforts to feel good about himself and his world. For example, facing the realization that failure in an important venture resulted from one's own inadequacies would be self-devaluating. Hence a person may tend to avoid facing this reality by rationalizing projecting, or using other defense mechanisms.

Similarly, a proud parent may screen out the fact that his son is drinking too much, or is unduly preoccupied with drugs and neglecting his studies; or the parent may attempt to minimize the undesirable behavior by saying that young people go through "phases" and that there is really no cause for concern.

While screening out unpleasant reality whether it relates to oneself or the environment- may help the individual feel adequate in facing life's problems, it may also keep him from making needed changes in his frame of reference and modes of adjustment.

4.   Fearfulness Vs positive action :   Although most people are familiar with the increased tension and desire to flee that accompany fear, few realize that fatigue, worry, indecision and oversensitivity my also be disguised manifestations of fear. The pervasive effects of fear are illustrated by the person who is afraid to go out in the dark alone after watching a terrifying murder mystery on television; if the person does go out anyway, he is prone to jump at the slightest sound. This increased sensitivity is characteristic of the many frightened, insecure persons who go through life overreacting to the slightest threat. Their fears rob them of courage and cripple their reasoning and other adjustive capacities.

Probably all of us experience some degree of fear in facing the problems of living. The brave person is not the one who experiences no fear, but the one who acts courageously despite fear. Not realizing this, many people expend their efforts trying to deny or conceal their fears, instead of learning to function effectively in spite of them.

Phobias may occur in a wide range of personality patterns and abnormal syndromes, reflecting the part that anxiety and avoidance play in many manifestations of abnormal behavior. In general, phobias have been thought of as attempts to cope with specific internal or external dangers by carefully avoiding situations likely to bring about whatever is feared. Thus phobias have been seen as simple defensive reactions in which the person feels he must give in to his fears in order to protect himself. This same view is applicable to phobic neurosis, although the focus has shifted from specific phobias to the more general role of phobias in an overall neurotic life-style of defensive and avoidant behaviors.

Three major causal patterns have been emphasized in the development of phobias : conditioning and avoidance learning, defense against threatening impulses, and the displacement of anxiety.

1. Conditioning and avoidance learning : As we saw in Watson's case of "little Albert"- who was conditioned to fear a white rat- a phobia may be the learned result of prior trauma in the feared situation. And this fear, as happened in the case of little Albert, may generalize to similar situations.

Phobias of this type are not difficult to understand because most of us probably have mild phobias based on previous learning. A person who has been attacked and bitten by a vicious dog may feel uneasy around dogs, even though some reconditioning experiences have intervened. A pervasive pattern of fear and avoidance behavior can be learned in much the same way. For example, if a child's fumbling attempts to master new skills are ridiculed by her parents, or if she is discouraged fro becoming independent, she may never develop the confidence she needs to cope with new situations. In effect, she learns that avoidance is the "appropriate" response where risk or uncertainty is involved.

2. Defense against threatening impulses : A phobia may represent a defensive reaction that protects the individual from situations in which his repressed aggressive or sexual impulses might become dangerous. Thus a husband may develop a phobia of lakes, swimming pools, and other bodies of water because on drowning his wife; similarly, a young mother may develop a phobia of being alone with her unwanted baby because of recurring fantasies about strangling him.

3. Displacement of anxiety : A phobia may represent a displacement of anxiety from some external threat that elicited it to some other object or situation.

With the help of above discussion, we may discuss our results in the following way-

The families are generally classified in two ways. One classification is joint families and nuclear families. The other classification is small families and large families. This latter classification is generally done for nuclear families.

Joint families :

This kind of family has a large number of members who are related to each other. Such families include parents, grandparents, uncles and aunts and their children too.

The head of the joint family is an authoritarian figure, who exerts authority over other members of the family.

The child has interpersonal relations with a large number of people. So the child learns easily how to behave in the society but these relations are not much intimate. They are superficial to a great extent.

There are many children in joint families. So the children have greater opportunity to mix with other children and imitate them. They come in contact with adults for a lesser amount of time. The mother generally is overburdened with work so the children have less chance to be in contact with the adults or experience the affection of the mother. So there is poorer language development as compared to the nuclear families. The emotional needs of these children also are not well satisfied.

But the older children from the joint families develop a greater sense of responsibility for at times they have to share the responsibility with the adults. The joint family consists of many adults. So discipline tends to be inconsistent. Some adults approve of a particular behavioral pattern while others do not approve of it.

Nuclear Families :

This kind of family consists of parents and their children. Father is the head of the family and the family atmosphere is generally not authoritarian.

The children cannot have interpersonal relationship with a very large number of persons, but the relationship that exists is not at a superficial level. It is quite intimate.

The nuclear family does not consist of many children so the children don't have on opportunity to mix with many children around, but they have a lot of opportunity to be in contact with the adults. They get grater love and affection of the mother. This helps in proper language and emotional development of the children. Language and speech development therefore is faster in the nuclear families.

Since the only adults in the nuclear families are the parents, there is a likelihood of more consistent discipline. The behavior that is approved by the mother is generally approved by the father too.

The present investigation results showed that the children coming from joint family were significantly high decisiveness, high responsibility, high emotional stability, high masculinity, high friendliness, high heterosexuality, high ego strength, high curiosity and high dominance than children coming from nuclear family.

Gender Differences

Obviously, males and females differ biologically in their genitals and other aspects of anatomy, and in their physiological functioning. These readily apparent physical disparities between males and females lead people to expect other differences as well. Recall from Chapter 6 the stereotypes are widely held beliefs that people posess certain characteristics simply because of their membership in a particular group. Gender stereotypes are widely shared beliefs about males' and females' abilities, personality traits, and social behavior. Research finds a great deal of consensus on supposed behavioral differences between men and women (Bergen & Williams, 1991). For example, a survey of gender stereotypes in 25 countries revealed considerable similarity of views (Williams & Best 1990).

The present investigation results showed that the male children were significantly high decisiveness, high responsibility, high emotional stability, high masculinity, high friendliness, high heterosexuality, high ego strength, high curiosity and high dominance than the female children.

Birth Order :

Adler's theory stressed the social context of personality development (Hoffman, 1994). For instance, it was Adler who first focused attention on the possible importance of birth order as a factor governing personality. He noted that firstborns, second children, and later born children enter varied home environments and are treated differently by parents and that these experiences are likely to affect their personality. For example, he hypothesized that only children are often spoiled by excessive attention from parents and that firstborns are often problem children because they become upset when they're "dethroned" by a second child.

In recent years, however, Frank Sulloway (1995,1996) has argued persuasively that birth order does have an impact on personality. Sulloway's reformulated hypotheses focus on how the Big Five traits are shaped by competition among siblings as they struggle to find a "niche" in their family environments. For example, he hypothesizes that firstborns should be more conscientious but less agreeable and open to experience than later-borns. In light of these personality patterns, he further speculates that firstborns tend to be conventional and achievement oriented, whereas later-borns tend to be liberal and rebellious. To evaluate his hypotheses, Sulloway reexamined decades of research on birth order. After eliminating many studies that failed to control for important confounding variables, such as social class and family size, he concluded that the results of the remaining well-controlled studies provided impressive evidence in favor of his hypotheses. Some subsequent studies have provided additional support for Sulloway's analyses (Paulhus, Trapnell, & Chen 199) but others have not (Freeese, powell, &Steelman, 1999) Harris, 2000) More studies will be needed, as research on birth order is enjoying a bit of a renaissance.

The present study results showed that the first born children   were significantly high decisiveness, high responsibility, high emotional stability, high masculinity, high friendliness, high heterosexuality, high ego strength, high curiosity and high dominance than the last born children.

1.   Decisiveness trait refers to person's ability to take quick decisions in controversial issues, to decide priorities and attend accordingly, to take clear-cut stand over the given issues, etc. The relationship between decisiveness and phobic reaction was negative. It indicates that the person having high decisiveness shows less phobic reactions. The result support the hypothesis.

2.   Responsibility is defined in terms of a number of behavioral syndromes such as finishing a task in time, meeting people on appointed time, going somewhere according to fixed schedule, attending meeting in time, etc. The relationship between responsibility and phobic reaction was negative. It indicates that the person having high responsibility shows less phobic reactions. The result support the hypothesis.

3.   Emotional stability persons having trait of emotional stability has well control over his emotion, talk confidently with others, consider ailments in their proper perspective, face comments and criticisms realistically, etc. The relationship between Emotional stability and phobic reaction was positive. It indicates that the person having high emotional stability shows high phobic reactions. The result does not support the hypothesis.

4.   Masculinity trait refers to person's ability to do arduous and risky work, his ability to handle challenges from military, taking interest in mountaineering, fighting etc. The relationship between masculinity and phobic reaction was zero. The result support the hypothesis.

5.   Friendliness persons possessing such trait develop deeper acquaintance with people, often help others in time of trouble and show proper love and affection to even juniors and unknowns. The relationship between friendliness and phobic reaction was negative. It indicates that the person having high friendliness shows less phobic reactions. The result support the hypothesis.

6.   Heterosexuality persons possessing such trait have normal sex relationship with opposite sex, don't feel shy among members of opposite sex and take active participation in working with members of opposite sex. The relationship between heterosexuality and phobic reaction was zero. The result support the hypothesis.

7.   Ego- Strength persons having the trait of ego-strength tend to concentrate and attend to different activities at a tie, have feelings of adequacy and vitality, have adequate control over impulses and tend to show high coordination between thoughts and actions. The relationship between ego strength and phobic reaction was positive. The result does not support the hypothesis.

8.   Persons having the trait of curiosity tend to explore the details of objects or things which are relatively new, tend to reach the destination in tie, tend to know the contents of talks of others or reactions of others toward oneself, etc. The relationship between curiosity and phobic reaction was negative. It indicates that the person having high curiosity shows less phobic reactions. The result support the hypothesis.

9.   Persons having the trait of dominance tend to dictate over others for their duty, tend to be the leader of the group, tend to settle controversy between rivals, tend to undertake the supervision of a difficult and complex task. The relationship between dominance and phobic reaction was zero. The result support the hypothesis.

Chapter VI
Summary, Conclusion, Suggestion & Recommendation

Phobic disorders are common disorders that typically have their onset in childhood or adolescence. They are unique among psychiatric disorders in that the main categories of phobias are distinguished by the nature of an external stimulus rather than by differences in symptoms or course. Thus, individuals who have an irrational fear of animals are diagnosed with specific phobia, whereas those fear is triggered by people are diagnosed with social phobia. However, the quality of each disorder is distinctive. For example, generalized social phobia is often a chronic condition whose effects can be so pervasive and enduring that they seem to merge inextricably with underlying personality.

Aim of the Study:

The present study aimed at to study the strength of association between personality & phobic reaction, and find out the effect of type of family, sex, & birth order on personality of children.

Objectives of the Study:

1. To examine the Correlation in between Personality and Phobic Reaction of school going Ss.

2. To examine the Decisiveness among Joint Family and Nuclear Family school going Ss.

3. To examine the Decisiveness among Male and Female school going Ss.

4. To examine the Decisiveness among first Born and Last Born school going Ss.

5. To examine the Responsibility among Joint Family and Nuclear Family school going Ss.

6. To examine the Responsibility among Male and Female school going Ss.

7. To examine the Responsibility among first Born and Last Born school going Ss.

8. To examine the Emotional Stability among Joint Family and Nuclear Family school going Ss.

9. To examine the Emotional Stability among Male and Female school going Ss.

10. To examine the Emotional Stability among first Born and Last Born school going Ss.

11. To examine the Masculinity among Joint Family and Nuclear Family school going Ss.

12. To examine the Masculinity among Male and Female school going Ss.

13. To examine the Masculinity among first Born and Last Born school going Ss.

14. To examine the Friendliness among Joint Family and Nuclear Family school going Ss.

15. To examine the Friendliness among Male and Female school going Ss.

16. To examine the Friendliness among first Born and Last Born school going Ss.

17. To examine the Heterosexuality among Joint Family and Nuclear Family school going Ss.

18. To examine the Heterosexuality among Male and Female school going Ss.

19. To examine the Heterosexuality among first Born and Last Born school going Ss.

20. To examine the Ego Strength among Joint Family and Nuclear Family school going Ss.

21. To examine the Ego Strength among Male and Female school going Ss.

22. To examine the Ego Strength among first Born and Last Born school going Ss.

23. To examine the Curiosity among Joint Family and Nuclear Family school going Ss.

24. To examine the Curiosity among Male and Female school going Ss.

25. To examine the Curiosity among first Born and Last Born school going Ss.

26. To examine the Dominance among Joint Family and Nuclear Family school going Ss.

27. To examine the Dominance among Male and Female school going Ss.

28. To examine the Dominance among first Born and Last Born school going Ss.

29. To examine the Phobic Reaction among Joint Family and Nuclear Family school going Ss.

30. To examine the Phobic Reaction among Male and Female school going Ss.

31. To examine the Phobic Reaction among first Born and Last Born school going Ss.

Hypothesis:

1. Correlation in between Decisiveness and Phobic Reaction of school going Ss will be negative.

2. There will be negative Correlation in between Responsibility and Phobic Reaction of school going Ss.

3. The relationship between Emotional Stability and Phobic Reaction of school going Ss will be positive.

4. Correlation in between Masculinity and Phobic Reaction of school going Ss will be insignificant.

5. There will be negative Correlation in between Friendliness and Phobic Reaction of school going Ss.

6. Correlation in between Heterosexuality and Phobic Reaction of school going Ss will be non significant.

7. There will be positive Correlation in between Ego strength and Phobic Reaction of school going Ss.

8. The relationship between Curiosity and Phobic Reaction of school going Ss will be negative.

9. Correlation between Dominance and Phobic Reaction of school going Ss will be non significant.

10. The Ss coming from Joint family have significantly high Decisiveness than the Ss coming from Nuclear family.

11. Male Ss have significantly high Decisiveness than the Female Ss.

213

12. First born Ss have significantly high Decisiveness than the Last born school going Ss.

13. Ss coming from joint family have significantly high Responsibility than the Ss coming from nuclear family.

14. Male Ss have significantly high Responsibility than the Female Ss.

15. First born school going Ss have significantly high Responsibility than the Last born school going Ss.

16. Joint family school going Ss have significantly high Emotional Stability than Nuclear family school going Ss.

17. Male school going Ss have significantly high Emotional Stability than the Female school going Ss.

18. First born school going Ss have significantly high Emotional Stability than the Last born school going Ss.

19. Joint family school going Ss have significantly high Masculinity than the Nuclear family school going Ss.

20. Male school going Ss have significantly high Masculinity than the Female school going Ss.

21. First born school going Ss have significantly high Masculinity than the Last born school going Ss.

22. Joint family school going Ss have significantly high Friendliness than the Nuclear family school going Ss.

23. Male school going Ss have significantly high Friendliness than the Female school going Ss.

24. First born school going Ss have significantly high Friendliness than the Last born school going Ss.

25. Joint family school going Ss have significantly high Heterosexuality than the Nuclear family school going Ss.

26. Male school going Ss have significantly high Heterosexuality than the Female school going Ss.

27. First born school going Ss have significantly high Heterosexuality than the Last born school going Ss.

28. Joint family school going Ss have significantly high Ego Strength than the Nuclear family school going Ss.

29. Male school going Ss have significantly high Ego Strength than the Female school going Ss.

30. First born school going Ss have significantly high Ego Strength than the Last born school going Ss.

31. Joint family school going Ss have significantly high Curiosity than the Nuclear family school going Ss.

32. Male school going Ss have significantly high Curiosity than the Female school going Ss.

33. First born school going Ss have significantly high Curiosity than the Last born school going Ss.

34. Joint family school going Ss have significantly high Dominance than the Nuclear family school going Ss.

35. Male school going Ss have significantly high Dominance than the Female school going Ss.

36. First born school going Ss have significantly high Dominance than the Last born school going Ss.

37. Joint family school going Ss shows significantly high Phobic Reaction than the Nuclear family school going Ss.

38. Female school going Ss shows significantly high Phobic Reaction than the male school going Ss.

39. First born school going Ss shows significantly high Phobic Reaction than the Last born school going Ss.

Sample:

After carefully studying location of the high schools, 10 high schools were selected from Aurangabad City. The Sample consisted of 800 Ss studying in 8th and 9th Std. The age range of the Ss was 13 to 15 years. The male female ratio was 1:1. At the second stage sample consisted of 400 Ss, only. It so happened, because at the second stage the nature of analysis of data was based on a 2 X 2 X 2 factorial design. In order to be included in the effective each S had to meet three criteria. At the first stage the Ss were classified in two groups (1) Joint family. (2) Nuclear family. In this process 125 Ss were deleted. Secondly, the Ss were classified on the basis of male female. In this classification 150 Ss were deleted. At the third Stage, Ss were classified on the basis of birth order i.e First born and last born. In this process 115 Ss were deleted. Lastly, to keep equal cell frequencies, 10 Ss were deleted randomly from the classified groups, where the number of Ss was more than fifty. Thus, at the second, the effective Sample of the present study consisted of 400 Ss.

Tools

Differential Personality Inventory (DPI):

This test is developed and standardized by L.N.K. Shinha and Arun Kumar Singh. The test consisted of 165 Items. The subjects were required to respond to each item in terms of 'True' OR 'False'. The test – retest Reliability Coefficient Range from .73 to .86 which were high and significant indicating that the Different dimensions of the Scale have sufficient Temporal Stability.

Neurosis Measurement Scale (NMS):

This test is developed and standardized by Dr. M.P. Uniyal and Dr. Km. Abha rani bisht. The test consisted of 70 Items and Five Alternatives. 'Always', 'Often', 'Sometimes', 'Rarely', and 'Never'. The reliability of the scale was determined by test-retest method. The retest was done after two different time intervals one month coefficient reliability .81 and 45 days coefficient reliability .79 and the scale has congruent validity with kundu's neurotic personality inventory.

Procedures of data collection

Each of the two instruments will be administered individuals as well as a small group. While collecting the data for the study the later approaches were adopted. The subjects were called in a small group of 20 to 25 subjects and their seating arrangements were made in a classroom. Prior to administration of test, through informal talk appropriate rapport was established. At first, differential personality scale was distributed to the Ss. they were asked to read the instructions given on the first page. After that they were asked to write the answers as fast as they can. Filled copies of scale were collected. After five minutes rest Neurosis Measurement Scale was given to the Ss. Following the same procedure whole data were collected.

Variable under study

Independent variable-

4. Types of family
5. Sex
6. Birth Order

Dependent Variable

1. Decisiveness
2. Responsibility
3. Emotional stability
4. Masculinity
5. Friendliness
6. Heterosexuality
7. Ego Strength
8. Curiosity
9. Dominance
10. Phobic Reaction

Design of Study:

In the present study joint family Vs Nuclear family, male Vs female, First Born Vs Last Born were treated is independent variables. Nine personality factor and phobic reaction were the dependent variables. Thus, a 2 x 2 x 2 balanced factorial design was used.

Statistical treatment of Data:

First the data were subjected to mean, standard deviation and correlation. Then three way analysis of variance was applied.

On the basis of the results following conclusions are drawn :

- ➢ Correlation in between Decisiveness and Phobic Reaction of school going Ss was negative.

- ➢ There was negative Correlation in between Responsibility and Phobic Reaction of school going Ss.

- ➢ The relationship between Emotional Stability and Phobic Reaction of school going Ss was negative.

- ➢ Correlation in between Masculinity and Phobic Reaction of school going Ss was be insignificant.

- ➢ There was negative Correlation in between Friendliness and Phobic Reaction of school going Ss.

- ➢ Correlation in between Heterosexuality and Phobic Reaction of school going Ss was non significant.

- ➢ There was negative Correlation in between Ego strength and Phobic Reaction of school going Ss.

- ➢ The relationship between Curiosity and Phobic Reaction of school going Ss was be negative.

- ➢ Correlation between Dominance and Phobic Reaction of school going Ss was non significant.

218

- The Ss coming from Joint family had significantly high Decisiveness than the Ss coming from Nuclear family.

- Male Ss had significantly high Decisiveness than the Female Ss.

- First born Ss had significantly high Decisiveness than the Last born school going Ss.

- Ss coming from joint family had significantly high Responsibility than the Ss coming from nuclear family.

- Male Ss had significantly high Responsibility than the Female Ss.

- First born school going Ss had significantly high Responsibility than the Last born school going Ss.

- Joint family school going Ss had significantly high Emotional Stability than Nuclear family school going Ss.

- Male school going Ss had significantly high Emotional Stability than the Female school going Ss.

- First born school going Ss had significantly high Emotional Stability than the Last born school going Ss.

- Joint family school going Ss had significantly high Masculinity than the Nuclear family school going Ss.

- Male school going Ss had significantly high Masculinity than the Female school going Ss.

- First born school going Ss had significantly high Masculinity than the Last born school going Ss.

- Joint family school going Ss had significantly high Friendliness than the Nuclear family school going Ss.

- Male school going Ss had significantly high Friendliness than the Female school going Ss.

- First born school going Ss had significantly high Friendliness than the Last born school going Ss.

- Joint family school going Ss had significantly high Heterosexuality than the Nuclear family school going Ss.
- Male school going Ss had significantly high Heterosexuality than the Female school going Ss.
- First born school going Ss had significantly high Heterosexuality than the Last born school going Ss.
- Joint family school going Ss had significantly high Ego Strength than the Nuclear family school going Ss.
- Male school going Ss had significantly high Ego Strength than the Female school going Ss.
- First born school going Ss had significantly high Ego Strength than the Last born school going Ss.
- Joint family school going Ss had significantly high Curiosity than the Nuclear family school going Ss.
- Male school going Ss had significantly high Curiosity than the Female school going Ss.
- First born school going Ss had significantly high Curiosity than the Last born school going Ss.
- Joint family school going Ss had significantly high Dominance than the Nuclear family school going Ss.
- Male school going Ss had significantly high Dominance than the Female school going Ss.
- First born school going Ss had significantly high Dominance than the Last born school going Ss.
- Joint family school going Ss showed significantly high Phobic Reaction than the Nuclear family school going Ss.
- Female school going Ss showed significantly high Phobic Reaction than the male school going Ss.

➤ First born school going Ss showed significantly high Phobic Reaction than the Last born school going Ss.

CPSIA information can be obtained
at www.ICGtesting.com
Printed in the USA
BVHW052055230123
656904BV00013B/177